OCCULTISM,
WITCHCRAFT,
and
CULTURAL
FASHIONS

Mircea Eliade

The University
of Chicago Press
Chicago
and London

OCCULTISM, *WITCHCRAFT,* and CULTURAL FASHIONS

Essays in Comparative Religions

91-538

The University of Chicago Press, Chicago, 60637
The University of Chicago Press, Ltd., London

© 1976 by The University of Chicago
All rights reserved. Published 1976
Printed in the United States of America
93 92 91 90 89 88   8 7 6

Library of Congress Cataloging in Publication Data
Eliade, Mircea, 1907–
    Occultism, witchcraft, and cultural fashions.

    Bibliography: p.
    Includes index.
    1. Religions — History.   2. Occult sciences.
I. Title.
BL80.2.E43   291   75-12230
ISBN 0-226-20391-3

To Giuseppe Tucci

In memory of our
discussions in
Calcutta, 1929–1931

Contents

Preface   ix

1 Cultural Fashions and History of Religions   1
2 The World, the City, the House   18
3 Mythologies of Death: An Introduction   32
4 The Occult and the Modern World   47
5 Some Observations on European Witchcraft   69
6 Spirit, Light, and Seed   93

Notes   120
Index   143

Preface

At a certain moment in his old age, a prolific author is bound to discover that many of his most cherished projected books remain unwritten. I do not know how others react to such a disquieting discovery, but, speaking for myself, it was with a melancholic resignation that I decided to abandon a number of works that were drafted and partially written over the past twenty-five years. As usually happens, however, I have from time to time made use of these notes and materials in the preparation of public lectures, addresses, and journal articles. Of course, such occasional essays do not sum up the results of long years of research, nor do they always present the many aspects of the topic under consideration in a consistent fashion. But they do have the advantage that, having been prepared for audiences largely composed of nonspecialists, they are accessible to any intelligent reader. All the risks involved in any attempt at "popularization" notwithstanding, this advantage must not be disregarded. In the last analysis, the scholar's only innocent ambition is to be read outside his own community of learning. For many reasons, which I have tried to discuss in some of my earlier publications, this ambition ought particularly to be encouraged among students in the discipline of history of religions.

I have thus selected the materials included in the present volume from several dozen lectures and articles written over the past ten years. All of them are, directly or indirectly, related to projected major works. Most of these essays have an introductory character;

their main intention is to recall some older but now neglected problems or to reopen well-known controversies from new or less familiar perspectives. With the exception of the last essay (chapter 6), all the pieces collected in this volume were originally delivered as lectures. I have not tried to change their oral style but have added notes and occasionally a few paragraphs by way of amplification.

Obviously, the last chapter—"Spirit, Light, and Seed"—contrasts somewhat with the rest of the essays. It was written for a learned journal, displays numerous documents from some less familiar cultures, and supplies copious bibliography in the notes. But such external (one is tempted to say: typographical) features should not delude the reader: this text does not pretend to be ranked among the products of pure erudition. The proliferation of quotations and critical references simply serves to acquaint the reader with some of the innumerable expressions of an archaic and widely diffused *theologomenon*, namely, the equation of the divine and "spiritual" mode of being with the experience of Pure Light and the equation of the divine creativity with a seminal iridescence. The subject is most fascinating, and it also has considerable importance for the problem of "universals" (or: "invariables") in the history of religious experience. Indeed, the equation Spirit = Light = divine (spiritual) creativity, when considered together with the morphology of luminous theophanies and experiences of "inner light," enables the historian of religions to identify a "universal" no less significant than the now well-known *mysterium tremendum*.

I am happy to thank my former students who have corrected and stylistically improved these texts: Professors Nancy Falk (chapter 1), Norman Girardot (chapter 2), and Park McGinty (chapter 6). I am particularly grateful to my assistant, Mr. Bruce Lincoln, for his care in correcting and editing chapters 3, 4, and 5. These pages, like my entire work of the past twenty-five years, could not have been written without the inspiring presence and uninterrupted support of my wife. But . . . "Whereof one cannot speak, thereof one must be silent."

Mircea Eliade
University of Chicago

1 Cultural Fashions and History of Religions

The Artist's Unsuspected Mythologies

The question that I should like to discuss in this paper is the following: what does a historian of religions have to say about his contemporary milieu? In what sense can he contribute to the understanding of its literary or philosophical movements, its recent and significant artistic orientations? Or even more, what has he to say, as a historian of religions, in regard to such manifestations of the *Zeitgeist* as its philosophical and literary vogues, its so-called cultural fashions? It seems to me that, at least in some instances, his special training should enable him to decipher meanings and intentions less manifest to others. I am not referring to those cases in which the religious context or implications of a work are more or less evident, as, for example, Chagall's paintings with their enormous "eye of God," their angels, severed heads, and bodies flying upside down—and his omnipresent ass, that messianic animal par excellence. Or Ionesco's recent play, *Le Roi se meurt*, which cannot be fully understood if one does not know the *Tibetan Book of*

A public lecture given at the University of Chicago in October 1965 and published in *The History of Religions: Essays on the Problem of Understanding*, edited by Joseph M. Kitagawa, with the collaboration of Mircea Eliade and Charles H. Long (Chicago: University of Chicago Press, 1967), pp. 20–38.

the Dead and the *Upanishads*. (And I can testify to the fact that
Ionesco *did* read these texts; but the important thing for us to
determine is what he accepted and what he ignored or rejected.
Thus it is not a question of searching for *sources*, but a more
exciting endeavor: to examine the renewal of Ionesco's imaginary
creative universe through his encounter with exotic and traditional
religious universes.)

But there are instances when only a historian of religions can
discover some secret significance of a cultural creation, whether
ancient or contemporary. For example, only a historian of religions
is likely to perceive that there is a surprising structural analogy
between James Joyce's *Ulysses* and certain Australian myths of the
totemic-hero type. And just as the endless wanderings and fortui-
tous meetings of the Australian cultural heroes seem monotonous to
those who are familiar with Polynesian, Indo-European, or North
American mythologies, so the wanderings of Leopold Bloom in
Ulysses appear monotonous to an admirer of Balzac or Tolstoi. But
the historian of religions knows that the tedious wanderings and
performances of the mythical ancestors reveal to the Australian a
magnificent history in which he is existentially involved, and the
same thing can be said of the apparently tedious and banal journey
of Leopold Bloom in his native city. Again, only the historian of
religions is likely to catch the very striking similarities between the
Australian and Platonic theories of reincarnation and anamnesis.
For Plato, learning is recollecting. Physical objects help the soul
withdraw into itself and, through a sort of ''going back,'' to rediscover and repossess the original knowledge that it possessed in its
extraterrestrial condition. Now, the Australian novice discovers,
through his initiation, that he has already been here, in the mythical
time; he was here in the form of the mythical ancestor. Through
initiation he again learns to do those things which he did at the
beginning, when he appeared for the first time in the form of a
mythical being.

It would be useless to accumulate more examples. I will only add
that the historian of religions is able to contribute to the understanding of writers as different as Jules Verne and Gérard de Nerval,

Novalis and García Lorca.[1] It is surprising that so few historians of religions have ever tried to interpret a literary work from their own perspective. (For the moment I can recall only Maryla Falk's book on Novalis and Stig Wikander's studies of French writers from Jules Michelet to Mallarmé. Duchesne-Guillemin's important monographs on Mallarmé and Valéry could have been written by any excellent literary critic, without any contact with the history of religions.) On the contrary, as is well known, many literary critics, especially in the United States, have not hesitated to use the findings of the history of religions in their hermeneutical work. One need only call to mind the frequent application of the "myth and ritual" theory or the "initiation pattern" in the interpretation of modern fiction and poetry.[2]

My purpose here is more modest. I will try to see whether a historian of religions can decipher some hidden meanings in our so-called cultural fashions, taking as examples three recent vogues, all of which originated in Paris but are already spreading throughout western Europe and even the United States. Now, as we all know well, for a particular theory or philosophy to become popular, to be à la mode, *en vogue*, implies neither that it is a remarkable creation nor that it is devoid of all value. One of the fascinating aspects of the "cultural fashion" is that it does not matter whether the facts in question and their interpretation are true or not. No amount of criticism can destroy a vogue. There is something "religious" about this imperviousness to criticism, even if only in a narrow-minded, sectarian way. But even beyond this general aspect, some cultural fashions are extremely significant for the historian of religions. Their popularity, especially among the intelligentsia, reveals something of Western man's dissatisfactions, drives, and nostalgias.

"Totemic Banquets" and Fabulous Camels

To give only one example: Fifty years ago, Freud thought that he had found the origin of social organization, moral restrictions, and religion in a primordial murder, namely, the first patricide. He told the story in his book *Totem and Taboo*. In the beginning, the father kept all the women for himself and would drive his sons off as they became old enough to evoke his jealousy. One day, the expelled sons killed their father, ate him, and appropriated his females. "The totemic banquet," writes Freud, "perhaps the first feast mankind ever celebrated, was the repetition, the festival of remembrance, of this noteworthy criminal deed."[3] Since Freud holds that God is nothing other than the sublimated physical father, it is God himself who is killed and sacrificed in the totemic sacrifice. "This slaying of the father-god is mankind's original sin. This blood-guilt is atoned for by the bloody death of Christ."[4]

In vain the ethnologists of his time, from W. H. Rivers and F. Boas to A. L. Kroeber, B. Malinowski, and W. Schmidt, demonstrated the absurdity of such a primordial "totemic banquet."[5] In vain they pointed out that totemism is not found at the beginnings of religion and is not universal: not all peoples have passed through a "totemic stage"; that Frazer had already proved that, of the many hundred totemic tribes, only *four* knew a rite approximating the ceremonial killing and eating of the "totem-god" (a rite assumed by Freud to be an invariable feature of totemism); and, finally, that this rite has nothing to do with the origin of sacrifice, since totemism does not occur at all in the oldest cultures. In vain did Wilhelm Schmidt point out that the pretotemic peoples knew nothing of cannibalism, that patricide among them would be a

> sheer impossibility, psychologically, sociologically, and ethically [and that] . . . the form of the pre-totemic family, and therefore of the earliest human family we can hope to know anything about through ethnology, is neither general promiscuity nor group-marriage, neither of which, according to the verdict of the leading anthropologists, ever existed at all.[6]

Freud was not in the least troubled by such objections, and this wild "gothic novel," *Totem and Taboo*, has since become one of the minor gospels of three generations of the Western intelligentsia.

Of course, the genius of Freud and the merits of psychoanalysis ought not to be judged by the horror stories presented as objective historical fact in *Totem and Taboo*. But it is highly significant that such frantic hypotheses could be acclaimed as sound scientific theory in spite of all the criticism marshaled by the major anthropologists of the century. What lay behind this victory was first the victory of psychoanalysis itself over the older psychologies and then its emergence (for many other reasons) as a cultural fashion. After 1920, then, the Freudian ideology was taken for granted in its entirety. A fascinating book could be written about the significance of the incredible success of this "roman noir frénétique," *Totem and Taboo*. Using the very tools and method of modern psychoanalysis, we can lay open some tragic secrets of the modern Western intellectual: for example, his profound dissatisfaction with the worn-out forms of historical Christianity and his desire to violently rid himself of his forefathers' faith, accompanied by a strange sense of guilt, as if he himself had killed a God in whom he could not believe but whose absence he could not bear. For this reason I have said that a cultural fashion is immensely significant, no matter what its objective value may be; the success of certain ideas or ideologies reveals to us the spiritual and existential situation of all those for whom these ideas or ideologies constitute a kind of soteriology.

Of course, there are fashions in other sciences, even in the discipline of history of religions, though evidently they are less glamorous than the vogue enjoyed by *Totem and Taboo*. That our fathers and grandfathers were fascinated by *The Golden Bough* is a comprehensible, and rather honorable, fact. What is less comprehensible, and can be explained only as a fashion, is the fact that between 1900 and 1920 almost all the historians of religions were searching for mother-goddesses, corn-mothers, and vegetation demons—and of course they found them everywhere, in all the religions and folklores of the world. This search for the Mother—mother earth, tree-mother, corn-mother, and so on—and also for other demonic beings related to vegetation and agriculture is also significant for our understanding of the unconscious nostalgias of the Western intellectual at the beginning of the century.

But let me remind you of another example of the power and prestige of fashions in history of religions. This time there is neither god nor goddess involved, neither corn-mother nor vegetation spirit, but an animal—specifically, a camel. I am referring to the famous sacrifice of a camel described by a certain Nilus who lived in the second part of the fourth century. While he was living as a monk in the monastery of Mount Sinai, the Bedouin Arabs raided the monastery. Nilus was thus able to observe at first hand the life and beliefs of the Bedouins, and he recorded many such observations in his treatise *The Slaying of the Monks on Mount Sinai.* Particularly dramatic is his description of the sacrifice of a camel, "offered," he says, "to the Morning Star." Bound upon a rude altar of piled-up stones, the camel is cut to pieces and devoured raw by the worshipers—devoured with such haste, Nilus adds, "that in the short interval between the rise of the Day Star, which marked the hour for the service to begin, and the disappearance of its rays before the rising sun, the entire camel, body and bones, skin, blood and entrails, is wholly devoured."[7] J. Wellhausen was the first to relate this sacrifice in his *Reste arabischen Heiden-thumes* (1887). But it was William Robertson Smith who established, so to speak, the unique scientific prestige of Nilus' camel. He refers to this sacrifice innumerable times in his *Lectures on the Religions of the Semites* (1889), considering it "the oldest known form of Arabian sacrifice,"[8] and he speaks of the "direct evidence of Nilus as to the habits of the Arabs of the Sinaitic desert."[9] From then on, all the followers of Robertson Smith's theory of sacrifice—S. Reinach, A. Wendel, A. S. Cook, S. H. Hooke—abundantly and untiringly referred to Nilus' account. It is still more curious that even those scholars who did not accept Robertson Smith's theory could not—or dared not—discuss the general problem of sacrifice without duly relating Nilus' story.[10] In fact, no one seemed to doubt the authenticity of Nilus' testimony, even though a great number of scholars rejected Robertson Smith's interpretation of it. Thus, by the beginning of this century Nilus' camel had become so exasperatingly omnipresent in the writings of historians of religions, Old Testament scholars, sociologists, and ethnologists that G. Foucard declared, in his book *Histoire des religions et méthode comparative,*

It seems that no author has any longer the right to treat of history of religions if he does not speak respectfully of this anecdote. For it is indeed an anecdote . . . , a detail related as an "aside"; and on a unique fact, so slender, one cannot really build up a religious theory valid for all humanity.[11]

With great intellectual courage, Foucard summed up his methodological position:

Concerning Nilus' camel, I persist in the belief that it does not deserve to carry on its back the weight of the origins of a part of the history of religions.[12]

Foucard was right. Meticulous textual and historical analysis has proved that Nilus was not the author of the treatise *The Slaying of the Monks on Mount Sinai*, that this is a pseudonymous work, probably written in the fourth or fifth century, and, what is more important, that the text is full of literary clichés borrowed from Hellenistic novels; for example, the description of the killing and devouring of the camel—"'hacking off pieces of the quivering flesh and devouring the entire animal, body and bones''—has no ethnological value but reveals only a knowledge of the rhetorical-pathetic genre of these novels. Nonetheless, although these facts were already known soon after the First World War, thanks especially to Karl Heussi's painstaking analysis,[13] Nilus' camel still haunts many recent scientific works.[14] And no wonder. This short and colorful description of what is presumed to be the original form of sacrifice and the beginnings of religious communion was tailor-made to gratify all tastes and inclinations. Nothing could be more flattering to Western intellectuals, convinced, as so many of them were, that prehistoric and primitive man was very nearly a beast of prey and consequently that the origin of religion should reflect a troglodytic psychology and behavior. Furthermore, the communal devouring of a camel could not but substantiate the claim of many sociologists that religion is merely a social fact, if not just the hypostatic projection of the society itself. Even those scholars who called themselves Christians were somehow happy with Nilus' account. They would readily point out the immense distance that separates the total consumption of a camel—bones and skin included—from the highly spiritualized, if not merely symbolic, Christian sacraments. The splendid superiority of monotheism and especially of Christianity as over against all preceding pagan creeds and faiths could not be more convincingly evident. And, of course, all these scholars, Christians as well as agnostics or atheists, were supremely proud and happy to be what they were: civilized Westerners and champions of infinite progress.

I do not doubt that the anlysis of the three recent cultural fashions which I referred to at the beginning of this paper will prove no less revealing for us, although they are not directly related to history of religions. Of course, they are not to be considered equally significant. One of them, at least, may very soon become obsolete. For our purposes, it does not matter. What matters is the fact that during the past four or five years—the early 1960s—Paris has been dominated—one might almost say conquered—by a magazine called *Planète* and by two authors, Teilhard de Chardin and Claude Lévi-Strauss. I hasten to add that I do not intend to discuss here the theories of Teilhard and Lévi-Strauss. What interests me is their amazing popularity, and I will refer to their ideas only insofar as they may explain the reasons for that popularity.

A Magazine Called *Planète*

For obvious reasons, I shall begin with the magazine *Planète*. As a matter of fact, I am not the first to have pondered the cultural meaning of its unheard-of popularity. Some time ago the well-known and extremely serious Parisian paper *Le Monde* devoted two long articles to this very problem, the unexpected and incredible success of *Planète*. Indeed, some 80,000 subscribers and 100,000 buyers of a rather expensive magazine constitute a unique phenomenon in France—and a problem for the sociology of culture. Its editors are Louis Pauwels, a writer and a former disciple of Gurdjiev, and Jacques Bergier, a very popular scientific journalist. In 1961 they published a voluminous book, *Le Matin des sorciers*, which rapidly became a best-seller. In fact *Planète* was launched with the royalties earned by *Le Matin des sorciers*. The book has also been translated into English, but it has not made a comparable impact on the Anglo-American public. It is a curious mélange of popular science, occultism, astrology, science fiction, and spiritual techniques. But it is more than that. It tacitly pretends to reveal innumerable vital secrets—of our universe, of the Second World War, of lost civilizations, of Hitler's obsession with astrology, and so on. Both authors are well read, and, as I have already said, Jacques Bergier has a scientific background. Consequently, the reader is convinced that he is being given *facts*, or at least responsible hypotheses—that, in any case, he is not being misled. *Planète* is constructed on the same premises and follows the same pattern: there are articles on the probability of inhabited planets, new forms of psychological warfare, the perspectives of *l'amour moderne*, H. P. Lovecraft and American science fiction, the "real" keys to the understanding of Teilhard de Chardin, the mysteries of the animal world, and so on.

Now, in order to understand the unexpected success of both the book and the magazine, one should recall the French cultural milieu of the late 1950s. As is well known, existentialism became extremely popular immediately after the liberation. J.-P. Sartre, Camus, Simone de Beauvoir, were the guides and models inspiring the new generation. Sartre in particular enjoyed a popularity equaled by no other French writer since the days of Voltaire and Diderot, Victor Hugo, or Zola during the Dreyfus affair. Marxism itself had not become a real attraction for the young intellectuals before Sartre proclaimed his own Communist sympathies. Very little was left of the French Catholic renaissance of the early 1920s. Jacques Maritain and the neo-Thomists had already gone out of fashion at the beginning of the Second World War. The only living movements within Catholicism, aside from the Christian existentialism of Gabriel Marcel, were those which produced at that time the rather modest group of *Études Carmélitaines* (stressing the importance of mystical experience and encouraging the study of the psychology of religion and of symbolism) and the *Sources Chrétiennes*, with their reevaluation of Greek patristics and their insistence on liturgical renewal. But, of course, these Catholic movements had neither the glamor of Sartre's existentialism nor the charisma of communism. The cultural milieu, from philosophy and political ideology to literature, art, cinema, and journalism, was dominated by a few ideas and a number of clichés: the absurdity of human existence, estrangement, commitment, situation, historical moment, and so on. It is true that Sartre spoke constantly of freedom; but in the end *that* freedom was meaningless. In the late 1950s the Algerian war prompted a profound malaise among the intellectuals. Whether existentialists, Marxists, or liberal Catholics, they had to make personal decisions. For many years the French intellectual was forced to live almost exclusively in his "historical moment," as Sartre had taught that any responsible individual should do.

In this gloomy, tedious, and somehow provincial atmosphere— for it seemed that only Paris, or rather Saint-Germain-des-Prés, and now Algeria, really counted in the world—the appearance of *Planète* had the effect of a bombshell. The general orientation, the problems discussed, the language—all were different. There was no longer the excessive preoccupation with one's own existential "situation" and historical "commitment" but a grandiose overture toward a wonderful world: the future organization of the planet, the unlimited possibilities of man, the mysterious universe into which we are ready to penetrate, and so on. It was not the scientific approach as such that stirred this collective enthusiasm but the charismatic impact of "the latest scientific developments" and the proclamation of their imminent triumphs. Of course, as I have said already, science was supplemented with hermeticism, science fiction, and political and cultural news. But what was new and exhilarating for the French reader was the optimistic and holistic outlook which coupled science with esoterism and presented a living, fascinating, and mysterious cosmos, in which human life again became meaningful and promised an endless perfectibility. Man was no longer condemned to a rather dreary *condition humaine*; instead he was called both to conquer his physical universe and to unravel the other, enigmatic universes revealed by the occultists and gnostics. But in contrast to all previous gnostic and esoteric schools and movements, *Planète* did not disregard the social and political problems of the contemporary world. In sum, it propagated a *saving* science: scientific information which was at the same time soteriological. Man was no longer estranged and useless in an absurd world, into which he had come by accident and to no purpose.

The Cultural Significance of Teilhard's Popularity

I must stop here with my rapid analysis of the reasons for *Planète*'s success, for I realize that many of the things which I have said in connection with this magazine can be applied almost identically to the vogue of Teilhard de Chardin. It should be unnecessary to add that I am not speaking of the scientific and philosophic merits of Teilhard, which are unquestionable, but of the tremendous success of his books, all of which, as is well known, were published posthumously. And it is a strange paradox that the only Roman Catholic thinker who has gained a responsible and massive audience was prevented by his ecclesiastical authorities from publishing those very books which today are best-sellers in both the Old World and the New. What is even more important, at least one hundred volumes and many thousands of articles have been published all over the world, in less than ten years, discussing, in most cases sympathetically, Teilhard de Chardin's ideas. If we take into consideration the fact that not even the most popular philosopher of this generation, J.-P. Sartre, attained so massive a response after twenty-five years of activity, we must acknowledge the *cultural* significance of Teilhard's success. We have no books at all, and only a very few articles, about the ideas of Louis Pauwels and Jacques Bergier (both articles in *Le Monde* are concerned with the popularity of their magazine, *Planète*), but the majority of books and articles written about Teilhard discuss his philosophy and his religious conceptions.

Probably the readers of *Planète* and of Teilhard de Chardin are not the same, but they have many things in common. To begin with, all of them are tired of existentialism and Marxism, tired of continual talk about history, the historical condition, the historical

moment, commitment, and so on. The readers of both Teilhard and
Planète are not so much interested in history as in *nature* and in *life*.
Teilhard himself considers history to be only a modest segment in a
glorious cosmic process which started with the appearance of life
and which will continue for billions and billions of years, until the
last of the galaxies hears the proclamation of Christ as Logos. Both
the ideology of *Planète* and the philosophy of Teilhard de Chardin
are fundamentally optimistic. As a matter of fact, Teilhard is the
first philosopher since Bergson who has dared to express faith and
confidence both in life and in man. And when critics attempt to
prove that Teilhard's basic conceptions are not a legitimate part of
the Christian tradition, they usually point to his optimism, his belief
in a meaningful and infinite evolution, and his ignoring of original
sin and evil in general.

But, on the other hand, the agnostic scientists who read Teilhard
admit that for the first time they have understood what it can mean
to be a religious man, to believe in God and even in Jesus Christ
and in the sacraments. It is a fact that Teilhard has been the first
Christian author to present his faith in terms accessible and meaningful to the agnostic scientist and to the religiously illiterate in
general. For the first time in this century the agnostic and atheistic
masses of scientifically educated Europeans know what a Christian
is speaking about. This is not due to the fact that Teilhard is a
scientist. Before him there were many great scientists who did not
conceal their Christian faith. What is new in Teilhard, and explains
his popularity at least in part, is the fact that he has grounded his
Christian faith in a scientific study and understanding of nature and
of life. He speaks of the "spiritual power of matter" and confesses
an "overwhelming sympathy for all that stirs within the dark mass
of matter." This *love* of Teilhard's for the cosmic substance and the
cosmic life seems to impress scientists greatly. He candidly admits
that he had always been a "pantheist" by temperament and "less a
child of heaven than a son of earth." Even the most refined and
abstruse scientific tools—the electronic computer, for example—
are exalted by Teilhard because he considers them to be auxiliaries
and promoters of life.

But one cannot speak simply of the "vitalism" of Teilhard, for he is a religious man, and life for him is *sacred*; moreover, the cosmic matter as such is susceptible of being sanctified in its totality. At least this seems to be the meaning of that beautiful text entitled ''The Mass on the Top of the World.'' When Teilhard speaks of the penetration of the galaxies by the cosmic Logos, even the most fantastic exaltation of the bodhisattvas seems modest and unimaginative by comparison. Because for Teilhard the galaxies in which Christ will be preached millions of years hence are *real*, are living matter. They are not illusory and not even ephemeral. In an article in the magazine *Psyché*, Teilhard once confessed that he simply could not believe in a catastrophic end of the world—not now, and not after billions of years; he could not even believe in the second law of thermodynamics. For him the universe was real, alive, meaningful, creative, sacred—and, if not eternal in the philosophical sense, at least of infinite duration.

We can now understand the reason for Teilhard's immense popularity: he is not only setting up a bridge between science and Christianity; he is not only presenting an optimistic view of cosmic and human evolution and insisting particularly on the exceptional value of the human mode of being in the universe; *he is also revealing the ultimate sacrality of nature and of life*. Modern man is not only estranged from himself; he is also estranged from nature. And of course one cannot go back to a ''cosmic religion'' already out of fashion in the time of the prophets and later persecuted and suppressed by the Christians. One cannot even go back to a romantic or bucolic approach to nature. But the nostalgia for a lost mystical solidarity with nature still haunts Western man. And Teilhard has laid open for him an unhoped-for perspective, where nature is charged with religious values even while retaining its completely ''objective'' reality.

The Vogue of Structuralism

I will not say too much about the third recent vogue, that of Claude Lévi-Strauss, because it is interrelated with a broader interest in structural linguistics and structuralism in general. Whatever one may think of Lévi-Strauss's conclusions, one cannot but recognize the merits of his work. I personally consider him to be important primarily for the following reasons: (1) Although an anthropologist by training and profession, he is fundamentally a philosopher, and he is not afraid of ideas, theories, and theoretical language; therefore, he forces anthropologists to *think*, and even to think hard. For the empirically minded anthropologist, this is a real calamity, but the historian of religions cannot help but rejoice in the highly theoretical level on which Lévi-Strauss chooses to discuss his so-called primitive material. (2) Even if one does not accept the structuralist approach *in toto*, Lévi-Strauss's criticism of anthropological historicism is very timely. Too much time and energy have been expended by anthropologists in trying to reconstruct the *history* of primitive cultures, and very little on *understanding their meaning*. (3) Finally, Lévi-Strauss is an excellent writer; his *Tristes tropiques* is a great book, in my opinion his most important work. Furthermore, Lévi-Strauss is what I might call a "modern encyclopedist," in the sense that he is familiar with a great number of *modern* discoveries, creations, and techniques; for example, cybernetics and communication theory, Marxism, linguistics, abstract art and Béla Bartók, dodecaphonic music and the "new wave" of the French novel, and so forth.

Now, it is quite probable that some of these achievements have contributed to the popularity of Lévi-Strauss. His interest in so many modern ways of thinking, his Marxian sympathies, his sensitive understanding of Ionesco or Robbe-Grillet—these are not negligible qualities in the eyes of the younger generation of intellectuals. But in my opinion the reasons for Lévi-Strauss's popularity are primarily to be found in his antiexistentialism and his neopositivism, in his indifference to history and his exaltation of material "things"—of matter. For him, "la science est déjà faite dans les choses": science is already effected in things, in material objects. Logic is already prefigured in nature. That is to say, man can be understood without taking *consciousness* into consideration. *La Pensée sauvage* presents to us a thinking without thinkers and a logic without logicians.[15] This is both a neopositivism and a neonominalism, but at the same time it is something more. It is a reabsorption of man into nature—not, evidently, dionysiac or romantic nature or even the blind, passionate, erotic drive of Freud, but the nature which is grasped by nuclear physics and cybernetics, a nature reduced to its fundamental structures; and these structures are the same in both the cosmic substance and the human mind. Now, as I have already said, I cannot discuss Lévi-Strauss's theories here. But I would like to remind the reader of one of the most distinctive characteristics of the French "new-wave" novelists, particularly Robbe-Grillet: the importance of "things," of material objects—ultimately, the primacy of space and of nature—and the indifference to history and to historical time. Both in Lévi-Strauss, for whom "la science est déjà faite dans les choses," and in Robbe-Grillet we witness a new epiphany of "les choses," the elevation of physical nature to the rank of the one all-embracing reality.

Thus all three recent vogues seem to have something in common: their drastic reaction against existentialism, their indifference to history, their exaltation of physical nature. Of course, there is a great distance between the rather naïve scientific enthusiasm of *Planète* and Teilhard's mystical love for matter and life and his confidence in the scientific and technological miracles of the future, and there is an even greater distance between Teilhard's and Lévi-Strauss's conceptions of man. But what we might call their "worlds of image" are somehow similar: in all three instances we are confronted with a kind of *mythology of matter*, whether of an imaginative, exuberant type (*Planète*, Teilhard de Chardin) or a structuralist, algebraic type (Claude Lévi-Strauss).

If my analysis is correct, then the antiexistentialism and the antihistoricism patent in these fashions and their exaltation of physical nature are not without interest for the historian of religions. The fact that hundreds of thousands of European intellectuals are enthusiastically reading *Planète* and the works of Teilhard de Chardin has another meaning for the historian of religions than it might have for a sociologist of culture. It would be too simple for us to say that the terror of history is again becoming unbearable and that those European intellectuals who can neither take refuge in nihilism nor

find solace in Marxism are looking hopefully toward a new—
because scientifically approached—and charismatic cosmos. We
certainly cannot reduce the meaning of these vogues to the old and
well-known tension between "cosmos and history." The cosmos
presented in *Planète* and the works of Teilhard de Chardin is itself a
product of history, for it is the cosmos as understood by science and
in the process of being conquered and changed by technology. But
what is specific and new is the almost religious interest in the
structures and values of this natural world, of this cosmic substance
so brilliantly explored by science and transformed by technology.
The antihistoricism which we have identified in all three fashions is
not a rejection of history as such; it is rather a protest against the
pessimism and nihilism of some recent historicists. We even suspect a nostalgia for what might be called a macrohistory—a plane-
tary and, later, a cosmic history. But whatever may be said about
this nostalgia for a more comprehensive understanding of history,
one thing remains certain: the enthusiasts for *Planète*, for Teilhard
de Chardin, and for Lévi-Strauss do not feel the Sartrean *nausée*
when they are confronted with natural objects; they do not feel
themselves to be *de trop* in this world; in brief, they do not experience their own situation in the cosmos as an existentialist does.

Like all fashions, these new vogues will also fade out and finally
disappear. But their real significance will not be invalidated: the
popularity of *Planète*, of Teilhard de Chardin, and of Claude
Lévi-Strauss reveals to us something of the unconscious or
semiconscious desires and nostalgias of contemporary Western
man. If we take into consideration the fact that somehow similar
intentions can be deciphered in modern art, the significance of these
recent vogues for the historian of religions becomes even more
startling. Indeed, one cannot fail to recognize in the works of a
great number of contemporary artists a consuming interest in matter
as such. I will not speak of Brancuşi, because his love for matter is
well known. Brancuşi's attitude toward stone is comparable to the
solicitude, fear, and veneration of a Neolithic man when faced with
certain stones that constitute hierophanies for him; that is to say,
they also reveal a sacred and ultimate reality. But in the history of

modern art, from cubism to *tachisme*, we have been witnessing a continuing effort on the part of the artist to free himself from the "surface" of things and to penetrate matter in order to lay bare its ultimate structures. I have already discussed elsewhere the religious significance of the contemporary artist's effort to abolish form and volume, to descend, as it were, into the interior of substance while disclosing its secret or larval modalities.[16] This fascination for the elementary modes of matter betrays a desire to deliver oneself from the weight of dead forms, a nostalgia to immerse oneself in an auroral world.

If our analysis is correct, there is a decided convergence between the artist's attitude toward matter and the nostalgias of Western man, such as they can be deciphered in the three recent vogues we have discussed. It is a well-known fact that through their creations artists often anticipate what is to come—sometimes one or two generations later—in other sectors of social and cultural life.

2 The World
The City
The House

Living in One's Own World

Years ago, one of my professors at the University of Bucharest had the opportunity to attend a series of lectures given by the famous historian Theodore Mommsen. At that time, in the early 1890s, Mommsen was already very old, but his mind was still lucid and harbored a memory that was astonishingly complete and accurate. In his first lecture, Mommsen was describing Athens during the time of Socrates. He went to the blackboard and sketched, without a single note, the plan of the city as it was in the fifth century; he then proceeded to indicate the location of the temples and public buildings and to show where some of the famous wells and groves were situated. Particularly impressive was his vivid reconstruction of the environmental background of the *Phaedrus*. After quoting the passage in which Socrates inquires where Lysias is staying, and Phaedrus replies that he is staying with Epicrates, Mommsen pointed out the possible location of Epicrates' house, explaining that the text states that "the house where Morychus used to live" was "close to the temple of Olympian Zeus." Mommsen continued by graphically mapping the route that Socrates and Phaedrus took as they walked along the river Ilissus, and he then indicated the

A public lecture given at Loyola University, Chicago, in February 1970.

probable place where they stopped and held their memorable dialogue at "the quiet spot" where the "tall plane tree" grew.

Awed by Mommsen's amazing display of erudition, memory, and literary insight, my professor was reluctant to leave the amphitheater immediately after the lecture. He then saw an elderly valet come forward and gently take Mommsen's arm in order to guide him out of the amphitheater. At this point, one of the students still present explained that the famous historian did not know how to go home alone. The greatest living authority on fifth-century Athens was completely lost in his own city of Wilhelminian Berlin!

For what I intend to discuss in this article I could hardly find a better introduction. Mommsen admirably illustrates the existential meaning of "living in one's own world." His *real* world, the only one that was relevant and meaningful, was the classical Greco-Roman world. For Mommsen, the world of the Greeks and Romans was not simply *history*, that is, a dead past recovered through a historiographical *anamnesis*; it was *his* world—that place where he could move, think, and enjoy the beatitude of being alive and creative. I do not really know whether he always required a servant to guide him home. Probably not. Like most creative scholars, he probably lived in two worlds: the universe of forms and values, to the understanding of which he dedicated his life and which corresponds somehow to the "cosmicized" and therefore "sacred" world of the primitives; and the everyday "profane" world into which he was "thrown," as Heidegger would say. But then, in his old age, Mommsen obviously felt detached from the profane, nonessential, and for him meaningless and ultimately chaotic space of modern Berlin. If one can speak of an amnesia with regard to the profane space of Berlin, one has also to recognize that this amnesia was compensated for by incredible *anamnesis* of all that concerned Mommsen's existential world, i.e., the classical Greco-Roman universe. In his old age, Mommsen was living in a world of archetypes.

Perhaps the closest parallel to this experience of feeling lost in an unknown, chaotic space is found among the Achilpas, one of the Australian Aranda tribes. According to their mythology, a divine

being called Numbakula "cosmicized" their territory, created their
ancestor, and founded their institutions. Numbakula fashioned a
sacred pole out of the trunk of a gum tree, climbed up to the sky on
it, and disappeared. This pole represents the cosmic axis, for it is
around it that the land becomes habitable and is transformed into a
"world." For this reason its ritual role is a considerable one. The
Achilpas carry it with them in their wanderings and decide which
direction to take according to the way it leans. This allows them, in
spite of their continual moving about, always to find themselves in
"their world" and at the same time to remain in communication
with the heaven into which Numbakula has vanished. If the pole is
broken, it is a catastrophe; in a way, it is the "end of the world"
and a regression into chaos. Spencer and Gillen relate a legend in
which the sacred pole was broken and the entire tribe fell prey to
anguish. The people wandered haphazardly for a time and finally
sat down on the ground and allowed themselves to perish.[1] This is
an excellent illustration of the necessity for "cosmicizing" the land
which is to be lived in. The "world," for the Achilpas, becomes
"their world" only to the degree that it reproduces the cosmos
organized and sanctified by Numbakula. They cannot live without
this vertical axis which assures an "opening" toward the transcendent and at the same time makes possible their orientation in
space. In other words, one cannot live in a "chaos." Once this
contact with the transcendent is broken off and the system of orientation is disrupted, existence in the world is no longer possible—
and so the Achilpas let themselves die.[2]

No less dramatic is the case of the Bororos of the Matto Grosso in
Brazil, which is brilliantly discussed by Claude Lévi-Strauss in his
book *Tristes tropiques*. Traditionally, the Bororo village was organized in a rough circle around the men's house and the dancing
ground; and it was also divided into four quarters by two axes—one
running north to south and the other east to west. These divisions
governed the whole social life of the village, especially its system
of intermarriage and kinship. The Salesian missionaries who first
dealt with this tribe thought that the only way to help them was to
persuade them to leave their traditional village and settle in a new

one. These charitable and well-meaning missionaries established what they thought to be a more convenient and practical village of rectangular huts set out in parallel rows. This reorganization completely destroyed the complex Bororo social system, which was so closely bound to the layout of the traditional village that it could not survive transplantation into a different physical environment. What was even more tragic was that the Bororos, in spite of their quasi-nomadic way of life, felt completely disoriented in the world once they were removed from their traditional cosmology depicted in the village plan. Under these conditions, they accepted any plausible explanation offered by the Salesians for their new and confusing universe.[3]

Ultimately, for the man of archaic society, the very fact of *living in the world has a religious value*. For he lives in a world which has been created by supernatural beings and where his village or house is an image of the cosmos. The cosmology does not yet possess profane, protoscientific values and functions. The cosmology, that is, the cosmological images and symbols which inform the habitable world, is not only a system of religious ideas but also a pattern of religious behavior.

The Cosmogonic Model of City-Building

But if living in the world for archaic man has a religious value, this is a result of a specific experience of what can be called "sacred space." Indeed, for religious man, space is not homogeneous; some parts of space are qualitatively different. There is a sacred and hence a strong, significant space; and there are other spaces that are not sacred and so are without structure, form, or meaning. Nor is this all. For religious man, this spatial nonhomogeneity finds expression in the experience of an opposition between space that is sacred—the only *real* and *really* existing space—and all other spaces, the formless expanse surrounding it. The religious experience of the nonhomogeneity of space is a primordial experience, comparable to the founding of the world. For it is the break effected in space that allows the world to be constituted, because it reveals the fixed point, the central axis for all future orientation. When the sacred manifests itself in any hierophany, there is not only a break in the homogeneity of space; there is also a revelation of an absolute reality, opposed to the nonreality of the vast surrounding expanse. The manifestation of the sacred ontologically creates the world. In the homogeneous and infinite expanse, in which no point of reference is possible and hence no *orientation* can be established, the hierophany reveals an absolute fixed point, a *center*.

So it is clear to what a great degree the discovery—that is, the revelation—of a sacred space possesses existential value for religious man; for nothing can begin, nothing can be *done*, without a previous orientation—and any orientation implies acquiring a fixed point. It is for this reason that religious man has always sought to fix his abode at the "center of the world." *If the world is to be lived in*, it must be *founded*—and no world can be born in the chaos of the homogeneity and relativity of profane space. The discovery or projection of a fixed point—the center—is equivalent to the creation of the world. Ritual orientation and construction of sacred space has a cosmogonic value; for the ritual by which man constructs a sacred space is efficacious in the measure in which *it reproduces the work of the gods*, i.e., the cosmogony.

The history of Rome, as well as the history of other cities or peoples, begins with the *foundation of the town*; that is to say, the *foundation* is tantamount to a *cosmogony*. Every new city represents a new beginning of the world. As we know from the legend of Romulus, the ploughing of the circular ditch, the *sulcus primigenius*, designates the foundation of the city walls. The classical writers were tempted to derive the word *urbs* ("city") from *urvum*, the curve of a ploughshare, or *urvo*, "I plough round"; some of them derived it from *orbis*, a curved thing, a globe, the world. And Servius mentions "the custom of the ancients [which decreed] that, as a new town was founded by the use of a plough, so it should also be destroyed by the same rite by which it was founded."[4]

The center of Rome was a hole, *mundus*, the point of communication between the terrestrial world and the lower regions. Roscher has long since interpreted the *mundus* as an *omphalos* (i.e., navel of the earth); every town possessing a *mundus* was thought to be situated in the center of the world, in the navel of *orbis terrarum*. It has also been rightly proposed that *Roma quadrata* is to be understood, not as being square in shape, but as being divided into four parts. Roman cosmology was based on the image of a *terra* divided into four regions.[5]

Similar conceptions are to be found everywhere in the Neolithic world and the Early Bronze Age. In India the town, as well as the temple, is built in the likeness of the universe. The foundation rites represent the repetition of the cosmogony. In the center of the town there is symbolically located Mount Meru, the cosmic mountain, together with the high gods; and each of the four principal gates of the town are also under the protection of a god. In a certain sense, the town and its inhabitants are elevated to a superhuman plane: the city is assimilated to Mount Meru, and the inhabitants become "images" of the gods. Even as late as the eighteenth century, Jaipur was built after the traditional model described in the *Śilpa-śastra*.[6]

The Iranian metropolis had the same plan as the Indian towns, that is, it was an *imago mundi*. According to the Iranian tradition, the universe was conceived as a wheel with six spokes and a large hole in the middle, like a navel. The texts proclaim that the "Iranian country" (*Airyanam vaejah*) is the center and heart of the world; consequently, it is the most precious among all the other countries. For that reason, Shiz, the town where Zarathustra was born, was regarded as the source of royal power. The throne of Chosroes II was constructed in such a way as to symbolize the universe. The Iranian king was called "Axis of the World," or the "World's Pole." Seated on the throne, in the middle of his palace, the king was symbolically situated at the center of the cosmic town, the Uranopolis.[7]

This type of cosmic symbolism is even more striking with regard to Angkor in Cambodia:

The city with its walls and moats represents the World surrounded by its chains of mountains and by the mythical oceans. The temple in the center symbolizes Mt. Meru, its five towers standing up like the five peaks of the sacred Mountain. Its subordinate shrines represent the constellations in their courses, i.e. the Cosmic Time. The principal ritual act imposed on the faithful consists in walking round the building in the prescribed direction, so as to pass in succession through each stage of the solar cycle, in other words to traverse space in step with time. The temple is in fact a chronogram, symbolizing and controlling the sacred cosmography and topography of the Universe, of which it is the ideal center and regulator.[8]

With some variations, we find the same pattern everywhere in Southeast Asia. Siam was divided into four provinces, with the metropolis in the middle; and in the center of the town stood the royal palace. The country was thus an image of the universe; for according to the Siamese cosmology, the universe is a quadrangle with Mount Meru in the middle. Bangkok is called "the celestial royal city," "the city of the Gods," and so forth. The king, placed in the center of the world, was a *cakravartin*, a cosmocrator. Likewise, in Burma, Mandalay was built, in 1857, according to the traditional cosmology, that is, as an *imago mundi*—quadrangular and having the royal palace in the center. We find in China the same cosmological pattern and the same correlation among cosmos, state, city, and palace. The world was conceived as a rectangle having China in the middle; on the four horizons were situated four seas, four holy mountains, and the four barbarian nations. The town was built as a quadrangle, with three gates on each side and with the palace at the center, corresponding to the Polar Star. From this center, the perfect sovereign was able to influence the whole universe.[9]

The House at the Center of the World

It is a mistake to think that this cosmological symbolism was restricted to palaces, temples, and royal capitals and that such symbols were intelligible only to the learned theologians and the rich and powerful sovereigns, administrators, and artistocrats. For ob-

vious reasons I have referred to some of the most famous examples
of architectural construction; but we find the same cosmological
symbolism in the structure of any house, hut, or tent of traditional
societies, even among the most archaic and "primitive."

As a matter of fact, it is usually not possible to speak of the house
without referring to the city, the sanctuary, or the world. In many
cases, what can be said of the house applies equally to the village or
the town. The multiple homologies—among cosmos, land, city,
temple, palace, house, and hut—emphasize the same fundamental
symbolism: each one of these images expresses the existential experience of *being in the world*, more exactly, of being situated in an
organized and meaningful world (i.e., organized and meaningful
because it was created by the supernatural beings). The same cosmological symbolism, formulated in spatial, architectonic terms,
informs house, city, and universe. To understand the symbolism of
a Dyak house, one must know the cosmogonic myth, namely, that
the world came into being as a result of a combat between two polar
principles, the supreme deity, Mahatala, and the primordial water
snake. For every house is a replica of the primeval exemplary
house: it is symbolically erected on the back of the water snake, its
roof corresponds to the primeval mountain on which Mahatala is
enthroned, and an umbrella represents the tree of life. In the same
way, the cosmological dualism characteristic of Indonesian religion, culture, and society is clearly seen in the structure of every
Indonesian house, with its ritually consecrated "male" and
"female" divisions.[10]

The traditional Chinese house is similarly informed by a cosmic
symbolism. The opening in the roof, called "window of heaven,"
assures communication with heaven. The Chinese applied the same
term to the opening at the top of the Mongolian tent. This term—
"window of heaven"—also means, in Chinese, "chimney." The
Mongolian tent is constructed with a central pole, which emerges
through this upper hole. This post is symbolically identified with
the "Pillar of the World," i.e., with the *axis mundi*. In many parts
of the world this *axis mundi* has been concretely represented either
by the central pillar that supports the house or in the form of

isolated stakes called "World Pillars." In other words, *cosmic symbolism is found in the very structure of everyday habitations.* The house is an *imago mundi.* Because the sky was conceived as a vast tent supported by a central pillar, the tent pole, or the central post of the house, was assimilated to the Pillars of the World and was so named.[11]

Similar conceptions are found among many North American Indian tribes, especially the Algonquins and the Sioux. Their sacred lodge, where initiations are performed, represents the universe. The roof symbolizes the dome of the sky, the floor represents the earth, the four walls the four directions of cosmic space. The ritual construction of the sacred space is emphasized by a threefold symbolism: the four doors, the four windows, and the four colors all signify the four cardinal points. The construction of the sacred lodge thus repeats the cosmogony, for the lodge represents the world. We may also add that the interdependence between the cosmos and cosmic time ("circular" time) was so strongly felt that in several Indian languages the term for "world" is also used to mean "year." For example, certain California tribes say that "the world is past" or that "the earth has passed" to mean that "a year has passed." The Dakotas say: "The year is a circle around the world," that is, a circle around the sacred lodge.[12]

Perhaps the most revealing example of house symbolism is that of the Fali, a people of the North Cameroun. The house is the image of the universe and consequently of the microcosm represented by man; but it reflects at the same time all the phases of the cosmogonic myth. In other words, the house is not a static construction but has a "movement" corresponding to the different stages of the cosmogonic process. The orientation of the separate units (the central pole, the walls, the roof), as well as the position of the tools and furniture, is related to the movements of the inhabitants and their location in the house. That is to say, the members of the family change their places inside the habitation in respect to the seasons, the time of day, and the various modifications of their familial or social status.[13]

I have said enough about the religious significance of human dwelling places for certain conclusions to have become almost self-evident. Exactly like the city or the sanctuary, the house is sanctified, in whole or in part, by a cosmological symbolism or ritual. This is why settling somewhere—by building a village or merely a house—represents a serious decision, for the very existence of man is involved; he must, in short, create his own world and assume the responsibility of maintaining and renewing it. Habitations are not lightly changed, for it is not easy to abandon one's world. The house is not an object, a "machine to live in"; *it is the universe that man constructs for himself by imitating the paradigmatic creation of the gods, the cosmogony.* Every construction and every inauguration of a new building are in some measure equivalent to a new beginning, a new life. And every beginning repeats the primordial beginning, when the universe first saw the light of day. Even in modern societies, with their high degree of desacralization, the festivity and rejoicing that accompany settling in a new house still preserve the memory of the festive exuberance that, long ago, marked the *incipit vita nova.*

Israel, the Sacred Land

I do not think that we can dismiss all these beliefs and experiences on the ground that they belong to the past and have no relevance for modern man. The scientific understanding of cosmic space—a space which has no center and is infinite—has nothing to do with the existential experience of living in a familiar and meaningful world. Even such a *history*-oriented people as the Jews could not live without a cosmological framework comparable to some of the patterns I have been discussing. The Jews also believe that Israel is located at the center of the world and that the foundation stone of the Temple in Jerusalem represents the foundation of the world. The rock of Jerusalem reached deep into the subterranean waters (*tehom*). The Temple was situated exactly above the *tehom*, the Hebrew equivalent of the Babylonian *apsu*, the primeval waters before Creation. The *apsu* and the *tehom* symbolize the aquatic chaos, the preformal modality of cosmic matter, and, at the same time, the world of death, of all that precedes and follows life. The rock of Jerusalem thus designates the point of intersection and communication between the lower world and earth. Moreover, this vertical image is homologized to horizontal space, as the lower regions can be related to the unknown desert regions that surround the inhabited territory; that is, the underworld, over which the cosmos is firmly established, corresponds to the chaos that extends beyond the city's frontiers.[14]

Consequently, Jerusalem is

> that one place on earth which is closest to heaven, which is
> horizontally the exact center of the geographical world and
> vertically the exact midpoint between the upper world and the
> lower world, the place where both are closest to the skin of
> the earth, heaven being only two or eighteen miles above the
> earth at Jerusalem, the waters of *Tehom* lying only a thousand
> cubits below the Temple floor. For the Jew, to journey up to
> Jerusalem is to ascend to the very crucible of creation, the
> womb of everything, the center and fountain of reality, the
> place of blessing *par excellence*.[15]

For that reason Israel is, as Rabbi Nachman of Bratislava puts it, the "real center of the spirit of life and therefore of the renewal of the world . . . , the spring of joy, the perfection of wisdom, . . . the pure and healing power of the earth."[16] The vital power of the land and the Temple is expressed in a variety of ways, and the rabbis often appear to vie with one another in contests of exaggeration. In the same sense, a rabbinical text asserts that "when the Temple was ruined, the blessing departed from the world." As the historian of religions Jonathan Z. Smith interprets this rabbinical tradition,

> The Temple and its ritual serve as the cosmic pillars or the
> "sacred pole" supporting the world. If its service is interrupted
> or broken, if an error is made, then the world, the blessing,
> the fertility, indeed all of creation which flows from the
> Center, will likewise be disrupted. Like the Achilpas' sacred
> pole . . . , the disruption of the Center and its power is a
> breaking of the link between reality and the world, which is

dependent upon the Sacred Land. Whether through error or exile, the severing of this relationship is a cosmic disaster.[17]

Contemporary Jewish scholars and writers as different as Chaim Raphael, David Ben-Gurion, Richard L. Rubenstein, and Jonathan Smith utilize similar cosmological images when they try to express what the Exile meant for the Jews. "While the exile is an event which can be located chronologically as after A.D. 70," writes Jonathan Smith, it is above all a thoroughly mythic event: "the return to chaos, the decreation, the separation from the deity analogous to the total catastrophe of the primeval flood."[18] The loss of Jerusalem, writes Chaim Raphael, meant more than the historical event of the Jews driven into exile: "God himself was in exile. The world was out of joint. The destruction was the symbol of it."[19] Of course, the "homeless God," the presence of God exiled, are images previously used by Rabbi Akiba in the first century; but it is highly significant that they are so popular today. Jonathan Eibschutz, an eighteenth-century Talmudist, writes: "If we do not have Jerusalem . . . why would we have life? . . . Surely we have descended from life unto death. And the converse is true. When the Lord restores the captivity of Zion, we shall ascend from death unto life."[20] It is striking that

> even among the so-called atheistic, secularist, deeply Marxist Zionists who founded the first *kibbutzim*, their religion of "land and labor" is a resurgence of the old language of a recovered center, of life shared with the land. Thus, for example, A. D. Gordon, understood by many to be the leader of the secular communitarians in the early twentieth century, describes their experience in a language resplendent with overtones of cosmic trees, world navels, and so forth: "It is life we want," writes A. D. Gordon, "no more, no less than that, our own life feeding on our vital sources, in the fields and under the skies of our Homeland. . . . We come to our Homeland in order to be planted in our natural soil from which we have been uprooted. . . . It is our duty to concentrate all our strength on this central spot. . . . What we seek to establish in Palestine is a new re-created Jewish people."[21]

Cosmic Religions and Biblical Faiths

I could easily multiply quotations, and, of course, I could add many comparable examples from other modern cultures. I have stressed Jewish cosmological symbolism because it is less familiar;[22] as a matter of fact, Judaism and, to a certain extent, Christianity are generally regarded as being almost entirely *historical*, that is, *time*-oriented, religions. The land of Israel, with Jerusalem and the Temple in the center, is a sacred country because it has a sacred history, consisting of the long and fabulous series of events planned and carried out by Yahweh for the benefit of his people. But this is true for many other religions, primitive as well as Oriental. The land of the Arandas, of the Dyaks, and of the Bororos is sacred because it was created and organized by supernatural beings: the cosmogony is only the beginning of a sacred history, which is followed by the creation of man and other mythical events.

I do not need to discuss here the similarities and differences between so-called primitive, *cosmic* religions and *historical*, biblical faiths. What is relevant for our theme is that we find everywhere the same fundamental conception of the necessity to live in an intelligible and meaningful world, and we find that this conception emerges ultimately from the experience of a sacred space. Now one can ask in what sense such experiences of the sacred space of houses, cities, and lands are still significant for modern desacralized man. Certainly, we know that man has never lived in the space conceived by mathematicians and physicists as being isotropic, that is, space having the same properties in all directions. The space experienced by man is *oriented* and thus anisotropic, for each dimension and direction has a specific value; for instance, along the vertical axis, "up" does not have the same value as "down"; along the horizontal axis, left and right may be differentiated in value. The question is whether the experience of oriented space and other comparable experiences of intentionally structured spaces (for example, the different spaces of art and architecture) have something in common with the sacred space known by *Homo religiosus*.

This is, surely, a difficult question—but *who* can be expected to offer an answer? Certainly not someone who is unaware of what sacred space means and who totally ignores the cosmic symbolism of the traditional habitation. Unfortunately, this is very often the case.

I would like to conclude by reminding you of that famous lawsuit which followed Brancuşi's first exhibition at the Armory Show in New York. The New York customs officials refused to admit that some of Brancuşi's sculptures—for example, *Mlle Pogany* and *A Muse*—were really works of art and so taxed them, very heavily, as blocks of marble. We must not be overly harsh in our judgment of the New York customs agents, for, during the subsequent lawsuit over the taxation of Brancuşi's works, at least one leading American art critic declared that *Mlle Pogany* and *A Muse* were mere pieces of polished marble!

Brancuşi's art was so new that, in 1913, even some art specialists could not *see* it. Likewise, the cosmic symbolism of sacred space is so old and so familiar that many are not yet able to recognize it.

3 Mythologies of Death: An Introduction

Myths on the Origin of Death

Evoking the different life-crises of an Australian male, W. Lloyd Warner writes:

> The personality before birth is purely spiritual; it becomes completely profane or unspiritual in the earlier period of its life, when it is classed socially with the females, gradually becomes more and more ritualized and sacred as the individual grows older and approaches death, and at death once more becomes completely spiritual and sacred.[1]

Whatever they may think of death, a great number of our contemporaries will certainly *not* agree that death is a "completely spiritual and sacred" mode of being. For most nonreligious men, death was emptied of any religious significance even before life lost its meaning. For some, the discovery of the banality of death anticipated the discovery of the absurdity and the meaninglessness of life. As an anonymous British psychoanalyst is reported to have said: "We are born mad; then we acquire morality and become stupid and unhappy; then we die."

A public lecture given at the annual Congress of the American Academy of Religion, Chicago, November 1973.

This last sentence—"Then we die"—admirably expresses the Western man's understanding of his destiny, but it is a somewhat different understanding from that found in many other cultures. There, too, men strive to pierce the mystery of death and grasp its meaning. We do not know of a single culture where such a sentence—"Then we die"—would not be taken for granted. But this flat assertion of human mortality is only a pretentious platitude when it is isolated from its mythological context. A coherent and meaningful concluding sentence would be: ". . . and *therefore* we die." Indeed, in most traditional cultures, the advent of death is presented as an unfortunate accident that took place in the beginnings. Death was unknown to the first men, the mythic ancestors, and is the consequence of something that happened in primordial time.[2] As one learns how death first appeared in the world, one comes to understand the cause of one's own mortality as well: one dies because such and such a thing took place in the beginnings. Whatever the details of this myth of the first death may be, the myth itself offers men an explanation of their own mortality.

As is well known, only a few myths explain the advent of death as a consequence of man's transgressing a divine commandment. Somewhat more common are the myths relating mortality to a cruel and arbitrary act of some demonic being. Such mythic themes are found, for instance, among Australian tribes and in the Central Asiatic, Siberian, and North American mythologies, where mortality is introduced into the world by an adversary of the Creator.[3] In contrast to this, among archaic societies, most of the myths explain death as an absurd accident and/or as the consequence of a stupid choice made by the first ancestors. The reader may recall numerous stories of the type of the "Two Messengers" or "The Message That Failed," which are especially common in Africa.[4] According to these stories, God sent the chameleon to the ancestors with the message that they would be immortal and sent the lizard with the message that they would die. But the chameleon paused along the way, and the lizard arrived first. After she had delivered her message, death entered the world.

Seldom do we encounter a more appropriate illustration of the absurdity of death. One has the impression that one is reading a page of a French existentialist author. Indeed, the passage from being to nonbeing is so hopelessly incomprehensible that a ridiculous "explanation" is more convincing because it is ridiculously absurd. Of course, such myths presuppose a carefully elaborated theology of the Word: God could not change the verdict for the simple reason that, once uttered, the words *created* reality.

Equally dramatic are the myths that relate the appearance of death to a stupid action of the mythic ancestors. For example, a Melanesian myth tells that, as they advanced in life, the first men cast their skins like snakes and came out with their youth renewed. But once an old woman, coming home rejuvenated, was not recognized by her child. In order to pacify the child, she put her old skin on again, and from that time on men became mortal.[5] Lastly, let me recall the beautiful Indonesian myth of the Stone and the Banana. In the beginning, the sky was very near to the earth, and the Creator used to let down his gifts to men at the end of a rope. One day he lowered a stone. But the ancestors would have none of it, and called out to their Maker: "What have we to do with this stone? Give us something else." God complied; some time later he let down a banana, which they joyfully accepted. Then the ancestors heard a voice from heaven saying: "Because ye have chosen the banana, your life shall be like its life. When the banana-tree has offspring, the parent stem dies; so shall ye die and your children shall step into your place. Had ye chosen the stone, your life would have been like the life of the stone, changeless and immortal."[6]

This Indonesian myth aptly illustrates the mysterious dialectics of life and death. The stone symbolizes indestructibility and invulnerability and consequently an indefinite continuity of the same. But the stone is also a symbol of opacity, inertia, and immobility, while life in general and the human condition in particular are characterized by *creativity* and *freedom*. For man this ultimately means spiritual creativity and spiritual freedom. Thus, death becomes part of the human condition; for, as we presently shall see, it is the experience of death that renders intelligible the notion of *spirit* and of *spiritual beings*. In sum, whatever was the cause of the first death, man became himself and could fulfill his specific destiny only as a being fully aware of his own mortality.

The elder Henry James, father of William and Henry, once wrote that "the first and highest service which Eve renders Adam is to throw him out of Paradise." This is, of course, a modern, Western view of that primordial catastrophe, the loss of paradise and immortality. In no traditional culture is death regarded as a blessing. On the contrary, in archaic societies one can still detect the idea of man's perenniality, that is, the conviction that man, though no longer immortal, could live indefinitely if only a hostile agent did not put an end to his life. In other words, a *natural* death is simply inconceivable. Just as the ancestors lost their immortality through accident or demonic plot, so a man presently dies because he falls victim to magic, ghosts, or other supernatural aggressors.

Nevertheless, in many archaic cultures, as the myth of the Stone and the Banana so gracefully suggests, death is considered a necessary complement of life. Essentially, this means that death changes man's ontological status. The separation of the soul from the body brings about a new modality of being. From this point on, man is reduced to a spiritual existence; he becomes a ghost, a "spirit."

Cosmological Symbolism of Funerary Rites

In many cultures there is the belief that the separation of body and soul brought forth through the first death was accompanied by a structural modification of the entire cosmos: the sky was removed and the means of communication between heaven and earth was broken (the tree, liana, or ladder connecting heaven and earth was severed, or the cosmic mountain was flattened). Henceforth, the gods are no longer easily accessible, as they were before; they now dwell far removed in the highest heaven, where only shamans or medicine men are able to reach them, doing so in ecstasy, which is to say, in "spirit."[7]

There is also the belief that, when man was first made, the Creator bestowed soul upon him, while the earth provided his body.

At the moment of death, these two elements consequently return to their sources: the body to earth, and the soul to its celestial author.[8]

Such analogies between cosmogony, anthropogony, and death indicate, so to speak, the "creative" virtualities of the act of dying. For it is well known among traditional societies that death is not considered *real* until the funerary ceremonies are duly completed. In other words, the onset of physiological death is only the signal that a new set of ritual operations must be accomplished in order to "create" the new identity of the deceased. The body has to be treated in such a way that it will not be magically reanimated and become an instrument of mischievous performances. Even more important, the soul must be guided to her new abode and be ritually integrated into the community of its inhabitants.

Unfortunately, we know very little of the religious symbolism of funerary ceremonies among archaic and traditional societies. We realize the degree of our ignorance when, by a piece of luck, a contemporary anthropologist has the opportunity to witness a funerary ritual and to have it explained to him. Such was the case with the Colombian anthropologist Reichel-Dolmatoff, who, in 1966, attended the burial of a young girl of the Kogi tribe of Sierra Nevada de Santa Maria. The description published by him is still insufficiently known; it certainly merits being summarized here.

After choosing the place for the grave, the shaman (*máma*) executes a series of ritual gestures and declares: "Here is the village of Death; Here is the ceremonial house of Death; Here is the womb. I will open the house. The house is closed, and I am going to open it!" Following this, he announces, "The house is open," and shows the men the place where they should dig the grave. At the bottom of the tomb they put small green stones, shellfish, and a snail shell. Then the shaman vainly tries to raise the body, giving the impression that it is very heavy; it is only on the ninth try that he succeeds. The body is placed with the head toward the East, and he "closes the house," which is to say, fills in the grave. There follow other ritual movements around the tomb, and finally all return to their village. The ceremony lasts about two hours.

As Reichel-Dolmatoff has remarked, an archeologist of the future excavating the tomb would find a skeleton with its head facing East, along with some stones and shells. The rituals and, above all, the religious ideology implied in the rituals would not be "recoverable" along with the rest. Moreover, for a foreign observer today, the symbolism of the ceremony remains inaccessible if he ignores the totality of Kogi religion. For, as Reichel-Dolmatoff has seen, the "village of Death" and the "ceremonial house of Death" are "verbalizations" of the cemetery, while the "house" and "womb" are "verbalizations" of the grave (this explains the fetal position of the body, lying on its right side). These ceremonies are followed by the "verbalization" of offerings as "food for the dead" and by the ritual of "opening" and "closing" the "house-womb." A final purification completes the ceremony.

Furthermore, the Kogi identify the world—womb of the Universal Mother—with each village, each cultic house, each dwelling, and each grave. When the shaman lifts the corpse nine times, it signifies the return of the body to its fetal state by passing through the nine months of gestation in reverse. And as the tomb is assimilated to the world, the funerary offerings receive a cosmic significance. Moreover, the offerings, "food for the dead," also have a sexual sense, for in myths and dreams, and in the ceremonies of marriage, the act of eating symbolizes the sexual act; consequently the funerary offerings constitute a semen that fertilizes the Universal Mother. The shellfish are charged with a very complex symbolism also, and one that is not simply sexual in significance. They represent the living members of the family, while the snail shell symbolizes the "spouse" of the deceased; for if the shell is not found in the tomb, a young girl, upon arriving in the other world, "will ask for a husband," which will provoke the death of a young man from the tribe.[9]

A Ritual and Ecstatic Anticipation of Death

We interrupt here the analysis so aptly carried forward by Reichel-Dolmatoff. Such an example shows how precarious our understanding is of the anthropocosmic symbolism informing any

traditional interment and, consequently, how little we know of the
religious dimensions of death and dying in archaic societies.
Nevertheless, we are assured of one fact, namely, that everywhere
in the traditional world death is, or was, considered a second birth,
the beginning of a new, *spiritual* existence. This second birth,
however, is not natural, like the first, biological birth; that is to say,
it is not "given" but must be ritually created. In this sense, death is
an *initiation*, an introduction into a new mode of being. And, as is
well known, any initiation consists essentially of a symbolic death
followed by a rebirth or resurrection.[10] Besides, any passage from
one mode of being to another implies necessarily a symbolic act of
dying. One has to die to the previous condition in order to be re-
born into a new, superior state. In the initiation rites of puberty
the adolescent dies to his natural, biological condition and comes
to life again as a cultural being; and from this time forward he
has access to the spiritual values of the tribe. During their
initiation, novices are considered dead and behave like ghosts.[11]
In such cases we witness a fairly veridical anticipation of death,
i.e., an anticipation of the mode of being of a spirit. Consequently, in some cultures there is the belief that only those who
have been properly initiated will obtain a *real* postexistence; the
others will either be doomed to a larva-like state or will fall victim
to a "second death."

It is not my intention to evoke all the important religious and
cultural creations occasioned by the confrontation with death. One
could discuss in great detail the cults of the ancestors and the heroes
or the beliefs and rituals concerning the collective return of the
dead, i.e., those periodic masquerades in which some scholars have
seen the beginnings of drama. Whatever one may think of the origin
of Greek tragedy, it is certain that the ceremonies celebrating the
periodic return of the dead gave rise to complex and dramatic
spectacles, which played a considerable role in many folk cultures.

Particularly creative were the ecstatic experiences of the shamans, that is, their journeys to heaven or the world of the dead.
Representing a momentary separation of the soul from the body,
ecstasy was, and still is, considered to be an anticipation of death.
Able to travel in spiritual worlds and to see superhuman beings

(gods, demons, spirits of the dead), the shaman contributed exten-
sively to the knowledge of death:

> In all probability, many features of "funerary geography" as
> well as some themes of the mythology of death are the result
> of the ecstatic experiences of shamans. The lands that the
> shaman sees and the personages he meets in his ecstatic journeys
> to the beyond are minutely described by the shaman himself,
> either during or after his trance. The unknown and terrifying
> world of death thus assumes form and is organized in accordance
> with particular patterns. Finally it displays a structure, and, in
> the course of time, becomes familiar and acceptable. In turn,
> the supernatural inhabitants of the world of death become
> *visible*; they show a form, display a personality, even a
> biography. Little by little the world of the dead becomes
> knowable. In the last analysis, the accounts of the shamans'
> ecstatic journeys contribute to "spiritualizing" the world of the
> dead, at the same time that they enrich it with wondrous
> forms and figures.[12]

There is also a marked similarity between accounts of shamanic
ecstasies and certain epic themes in the oral literatures of Siberia,
Central Asia, Polynesia, and some North American tribes.[13] Just as
the shaman descends to the underworld in order to bring back the
soul of a sick person, so the epic hero goes to the world of the dead
and, after many trials, succeeds in carrying back the soul of a dead
person, as in the familiar story of Orpheus' struggle to bring back
the soul of Eurydice.

Further, a great number of dramatic motifs in both myth and
folklore involve journeys to fabulous regions beyond the ocean or at
the ends of the world. Obviously, these mythic lands represent the
realm of the dead. It is impossible to trace the origin or "history"
of such funerary geographies, but directly or indirectly they are all
related to different views of the otherworld, the most familiar being
the subterranean, the celestial, and that of the land beyond the
ocean.[14]

I shall have more to say of such mythical geographies later, but
for the moment let me recall some other examples of what may be
called the "creative" understanding of death and the act of dying.

In fact, once having been interpreted as a passage to another, superior mode of existence, death became the paradigmatic model of all significant changes in human life. The platonic assimilation of philosophy to an anticipation of death became, in the course of time, a venerable metaphor. But this was not the case with mystical experiences, from shamanistic ecstasies to those experienced by the great mystics of the high religions. A Hindu as well as a Christian saint "dies" to the profane condition: he is "dead to the world"; and the case is the same with the great Jewish and Muslim mystics.

All these creative homologies—symbols and metaphors brought forth by setting up the act of dying as the paradigmatic model of any significant transition—emphasize the spiritual function of death: the fact that death transforms man into a form of spirit, be it soul, ghost, ethereal body, or whatever. But, on the other hand, such spiritual transformations are expressed through images and symbols related to birth, rebirth, or resurrection, that is, to a new and some-times more powerful life. This paradox is already implicit in the earliest interpretation of the act of dying as the beginning of a new mode of existence.

As a matter of fact, there is a curious ambivalence, if not a latent contradiction, in many ritual patterns of confronting death. The spiritualizing virtue of death may be enthusiastically exalted, but the love for the body and for incarnate life turns out to be stronger. While it is true, as Lloyd Warner has said, that an Australian man becomes at death "completely spiritual and sacred," this transfor-mation is not greeted with rejoicing. Rather, everywhere in Aus-tralia, when someone dies, there is a sense of catastrophic crisis. The wailing of women, the gashing of one's head to draw blood, and other manifestations of grief and despair reach a real frenzy. "The collective grief and wrath are controlled only by the certainty and the emphatic reassurance that the dead will be avenged." [15]

The Paradoxical Multilocation of the Departed Soul

Most of these contradictory ideas and behaviors are occasioned by the problem of the soul's localization. There is a widespread belief that the departed ones haunt their familiar surroundings, although they are supposed to be concurrently present in their tombs and in the netherworld. Such paradoxical multilocation of the soul is explained in different ways according to the different religious systems. Either it is asserted that a segment of the soul remains near the dwelling or the tomb, while the "essential" soul goes to the realm of the dead; or it is held that the soul tarries for some time in proximity to the living before ultimately joining the community of the dead in the netherworld. Notwithstanding these and other similar explanations, there is a tacit understanding in most religions that the dead are present concurrently in the tomb and in some spiritual realm. Such a conception, which is widely prevalent in the Mediterranean world, was duly accepted by the Christian Church. To be sure, we are dealing here with a popular, pre-Christian tradition, later admitted to the Church. But the same idea was shared by even the most rigorous theologians, such as Saint Ambrose of Milan. When his brother, Satyrus, died in 379, Ambrose buried him near the body of a martyr. And the great theologian composed the following funerary inscription: "Ambrose has buried his brother Manlius Satyrus at the left hand of a martyr; in return for his good life, may the moisture of this holy blood seep through to him and water his body." [16] Thus, in spite of the fact that Satyrus was supposed to be *now* in *heaven*, the martyr's blood could still operate on the Satyrus buried in the *tomb*. This belief in the bilocation of the dead has nothing to do with the Christian doctrine of the resurrection of the body; for, as Oscar Cullmann rightly points out, "the resurrection of the body is a new act of creation which embraces everything . . . ," and "it is tied to a *divine total process* implying deliverance." [17]

The almost universal conviction that the dead are present both on earth and in a spiritual world is highly significant. It reveals the secret hope that, in spite of all evidence to the contrary, the dead are able to partake somehow in the world of the living. As we have seen, the advent of death makes possible the mode of being of the spirit, but, conversely, the process of spiritualization is realized and expressed through symbols and metaphors of life. One is reminded of the reciprocal translation whereby the most important acts of life are seen in terms of death and vice-versa; for instance, marriage as death, death as birth, and so on. In the last analysis, this paradoxical process discloses a nostalgia and perhaps a secret hope of attaining a level of meaning where life and death, body and spirit, reveal themselves as aspects or dialectical stages of one ultimate reality. Indirectly, this implies a depreciation of the condition of pure spirit. Indeed, one could say that, with the exception of Orphism, Platonism, and Gnosticism, the Near Eastern and European anthropologies conceived the ideal man not as a uniquely spiritual being but as an incarnate spirit. Similar conceptions can be deciphered in some archaic mythologies. Moreover, one can point out in certain primitive millenarian movements the eschatological hope for the resurrection of the body, a hope shared by Zoroastrianism, Judaism, Christianity, and Islam.[18]

The paradox of the reciprocal translation of life symbols and metaphors with the symbols and metaphors of death has attracted the attention of some psychologists, linguists, and philosophers, but as yet (at least to my knowledge) no historian of religions has contributed significantly to the discussion. However, the historian of religions may be able to decipher meanings and intentionalities that have escaped other researchers. The paradox of this reciprocal translation reveals that, whatever one may think or may believe he thinks of life and death, he is constantly experiencing modes and levels of dying. This means more than just a confirmation of the biological truism that death is always present in life. The important fact is that, consciously or unconsciously, we are perpetually exploring the imaginary worlds of death and untiringly invent new ones. This also means that we are anticipating death experiences even when we are, so to say, driven by the most creative epiphanies of life.

Mythic Funerary Geographies

To illustrate, let us go back to the mythical funerary geographies discussed a few moments ago. The morphology of such fabulous realms is extremely rich and complex. No scholar can claim that he knows all the paradises, hells, underworlds and counterworlds (or antiworlds) of the dead. Neither can he assert that he knows all the roads to these wonderlands, though he may be certain that there will be a river and a bridge; a sea and a boat; a tree, a cave, or a precipice; and a dog and a demonic or angelic psychopomp or doorkeeper—to mention only the most frequent features of the road to the land-of-no-return.[19]

But what interests us is not the infinite variety of these fantastic lands but, as I said, the fact that they still nourish and stimulate our imagination. Moreover, new lands-of-no-return and new roads by which to reach them safely are continually being discovered, in our dreams and fantasies or by children, poets, novelists, painters, and filmmakers. It matters little that the *real* meaning of such lands and landscapes, persons, figures, and actions is not always clear to those who consider or imagine them. European and American children still play hopscotch, ignorant of the fact that they are reenacting an initiatory game, the goal of which is to penetrate and successfully return from a labyrinth; for in playing hopscotch they symbolically descend into the netherworld and come back to earth.[20]

Thus, the fact that mythologies of death and funerary geographies have become part of modern man's everyday life is both important and revealing. The French proverb, *Partir, c'est mourir un peu*, is often quoted, but it is not an illuminating example. Death is not anticipated or symbolically experienced only by such actions as going away, departing from a town or a country, and so forth. Neither everyday language, with its many picturesque evocations of hells, paradises, and purgatories, nor the many proverbs referring to them give full justice to the creative role played by the imaginary universes in modern man's life. Since the early '20s, literary critics have been successful in deciphering the mythologies and geographies of death in works of fiction, drama, and poetry. Historians of religions can go further and show that many gestures and actions of everyday life are symbolically related to modes and levels of dying. Any immersion in darkness, any irruption of light, represents an encounter with death. The same thing can be said of any experience of mountaineering, flying, swimming under water, or any long journey, discovery of an unknown country, or even a meaningful

encounter with strangers. Every one of these experiences recalls
and reactualizes a landscape, a figure, or an event from one of those
imaginary universes known from mythologies or folklore or from
one's own dreams and fantasies. It is needless to add that we are
seldom aware of the symbolic meaning of such experiences. What
matters is that, though unconscious, these symbolic meanings play
a decisive role in our lives. This is confirmed by the fact that we
simply cannot detach ourselves from such imaginary universes,
whether we are working or thinking, or relaxing and amusing ourselves, or sleeping and dreaming, or even vainly trying to fall
asleep.

Death as *Coincidentia Oppositorum*

We have repeatedly noticed the ambivalence of the images and
metaphors of death and life. In the imaginary universes, as in so
many mythologies and religions, death and life are dialectically
related. To be sure, there are also nightmares provoked by terrify-
ing funerary figures; but in such cases we are dealing with initiatory
experiences, though we are rarely aware of this fact. In sum, we
can say that even modern Western man, in spite of his religious
ignorance and his indifference to the problem of death, is still
involved, consciously or unconsciously, with the mysterious dialectic that obsessed our archaic ancestors. Death is inconceivable if it
is not related to a *new* form of being in some way or other, no
matter how this form may be imagined: a postexistence, rebirth,
reincarnation, spiritual immortality, or resurrection of the body. In
many traditions there is also the hope for a recovery of the original
perenniality. Ultimately this amounts to saying, if we may refer to
the Indonesian myth again, that the only satisfactory solution would
have been for the mythical ancestors to have chosen *both* the stone
and the banana. Separately, neither is able to meet man's paradoxical nostalgia for being fully immersed in life and, concurrently,
partaking of immortality—his yearning to exist alike in time *and* in
eternity.

For a historian of religions such paradoxical drives and nostalgias
are familiar. In a great number of religious creations we recognize

the will to transcend oppositions, polarities, and dualisms in order to obtain a sort of *coincidentia oppositorum*, i.e., the totality in which all contraries are abolished. To quote only one example, the ideal man is seen as androgynous and, as such, partaking of both life and perenniality.

The paradoxical conjunction of opposites characterizes, as is well known, the Indian ontologies and soteriologies. One of the most profound and most audacious reinterpretations of the Mahāyāna tradition, the Mādhyamika doctrine developed mainly by Nāgārjuna, went to the extreme limits of such dialectics. What could be more scandalous, even sacrilegious, than to proclaim, as Nāgārjuna did, that "there is nothing whatever to differentiate *saṃsāra* from *nirvāṇa*, and there is nothing whatever to differentiate *nirvāṇa* from *saṃsāra*"?[21] In order to set the mind free from illusory structures dependent on language, Nāgārjuna elaborated a dialectic leading to the supreme and universal *coincidentia oppositorum*. But his religious and philosophic genius was nourished by the venerable and pan-Indian tradition of paradoxical coincidences of being and nonbeing, eternity and temporal flux, beatitude and suffering.

To be sure, such grandiose Indian metaphysical creations cannot be ranked with the paradoxical drives and nostalgias that give birth to Western man's imaginary universes. However, their structural affinities are nonetheless evident, and they break open new and fascinating problems for philosophers and psychologists alike. On the other hand, we must keep in mind the recurrent efforts of the most profound and seminal Western thinkers to recover the existential meaning of death. In effect, though emptied of religious significations as a result of the accelerated secularization of Western society, death has become, since *Sein und Zeit*, the very center of philosophical inquiry. The exceptional success—one could almost say the popular vogue—of Heidegger's investigations illustrates the modern man's yearning for an existential understanding of death.

There is no point in trying to summarize the decisive contributions of Heidegger. But it is important to note that if Heidegger describes human existence as "Being-unto-death" (*Sein zum Tode*) and proclaims death as "the most proper, exclusive, and ultimate potentiality of *Dasein*,"[22] he also states that "death is the hiding-place where Being retreats as into a mountain stronghold (*Gebirg*)."[23] Or, to quote another passage, death, "as the shrine of Non-Being, hides within itself the presence of Being (*das Wesende des Seins*)."[24]

It is almost impossible to convey in a clear and simple formula any one of Heidegger's fundamental philosophical conclusions. Nevertheless, it appears that, for him, it is through the correct understanding of death that man takes possession of himself and consequently opens himself to Being. Indeed, an existence becomes authentic, i.e., fully human, when, comprehending the inevitability of death, man realizes the "freedom-unto-death (*Freiheit zum Tode*)." But inasmuch as death "hides within itself the presence of Being," one may interpret Heidegger's thought as indicating the possibility of encountering Being in the very act of dying. Whatever a Heideggerian exegete may think of such an interpretation, the important fact remains that Heidegger admirably proved the paradoxical coexistence of death and life, being and nonbeing.

A historian of religions would be particularly captivated by Heidegger's acute analysis of the multiform presence of death in the very core of life and of the inextricable camouflage of being in nonbeing. It is perhaps the historian of religion's privilege, and his highest satisfaction, to discover the continuity of human thought and imagination from prehistory to our own time, from a naïve and enigmatic myth like that of the Stone and the Banana to the grandiose but equally enigmatic *Sein und Zeit*.

4 The Occult and the Modern World

I must tell you, at the outset, just what I intend to discuss in this essay. I will try, first, to specify the sense of the terms "occult," "occultism," and "esotericism." I will retrace, afterwards, a short history of the interest in the occult, from the middle of the nineteenth century to our times. This retrospective view is necessary in order to appreciate the radical change we are witnessing in the contemporary Western world, especially in America. I will deal next with a number of secret practices, occult disciplines, and esoteric theories, mainly as they are publicized in the American youth culture. Within the limits of this essay, I am forced to make a rather severe selection among the many examples at our disposal. I will not take into consideration a number of significant phenomena, such as the new religious sects, spiritualist circles, parapsychological research, and so on. I must add that I will approach all these phenomena as a historian of religions, which is to say, I will not attempt to discuss their psychological, sociological, or even political contexts, meanings, or functions (leaving that to those who may be better qualified to do so).[1]

A paper delivered at the twenty-first annual Freud Memorial Lecture, held in Philadelphia on 24 May 1974 and published in the *Journal of the Philadelphia Association for Psychoanalysis* 1, no. 3 (September 1974): 195–213. Some additional material, chiefly bibliographical, has been included. Reprinted by permission.

According to the *Oxford Dictionary*, the term "occult" was first used in 1545, meaning that which is "not apprehended, or not apprehensible, by the mind; beyond the range of understanding or of ordinary knowledge." Almost a century later, in 1633, the word received a supplementary significance, namely, the subject of "those ancient and medieval reputed sciences, held to involve the knowledge or use of agencies of a secret and mysterious nature (as magic, alchemy, astrology, theosophy)." A more comprehensive definition of the "occult," corresponding to the contemporary usage of the term, was offered by Edward A. Tiryakian in his stimulating paper "Toward the Sociology of Esoteric Culture." "By 'occult,'" writes Tiryakian,

> I understand intentional practices, techniques, or procedures which: a) draw upon hidden or concealed forces in nature or the cosmos that cannot be measured or recognized by the instruments of modern science, and b) which have as their desired or intended consequences empirical results, such as either obtaining knowledge of the empirical course of events or altering them from what they would have been without this intervention. . . . To go on further, in so far as the subject of occult activity is not just any actor, but one who has acquired specialized knowledge and skills necessary for the practices in question, and insofar as these skills are learned and transmitted in socially (but not publicly available) organized, routinized, and ritualized fashion, we can speak of these practices as occult sciences or occult arts.[2]

The definition of "esotericism" is somewhat more delicate. Tiryakian understands, by "esoteric," those

> religio-philosophic belief systems which underlie occult techniques and practices; that is, it refers to the more comprehensive cognitive mappings of nature and the cosmos, the epistemological and ontological reflections of ultimate reality, which mappings constitute a stock of knowledge that provides the ground for occult procedures.[3]

But the most important and significant contemporary representative of esotericism, namely, René Guénon, strongly opposes so-called occult practices. As we shall see, this distinction is of consequence, and it will help us to understand the parallel roles of occultism and esotericism in modern times.

As is well known, all the beliefs, theories, and techniques covered by the terms occult and esoteric were already popular in late antiquity. Some of them—like, for instance, magic, astrology, theurgy, and necromancy—had been invented or systematized some 2,000 years earlier, in Egypt and Mesopotamia. It is useless to add that most of these practices did not completely disappear during the Middle Ages. However, they did recover a new prestige, becoming highly respectable and *en vogue* in the Italian Renaissance. I will come back to this point because, at least indirectly, it throws a certain unsuspected light on our topic.

Nineteenth-Century French Writers and Their Interest in the Occult

The vogue of occultism was created by a French seminarian, Alphonse-Louis Constant, born in 1810 and known by his *nom de plume*, Eliphas Lévi.[4] As a matter of fact, the term "occultism" was coined by this would-be priest and was used for the first time in English by the theosophist A. D. Sinnet in 1881. In his mature years, Lévi read the *Kabbala Denudata* of Christian Rosenroth and eventually the works of Jacob Boehme, Swedenborg, Louis-Claude de Saint-Martin ("le Philosophe Inconnu"), and other eighteenth-century *théosophes*. His books—*Dogme et rituel de la haute magie* (1856), *L'Histoire de la magie* (1859), and *La Clef des grands mystères* (1861)—met with a success difficult to understand today, for they are a mass of pretentious jumble. The "Abbé" Lévi was "initiated" into a number of secret societies—the Rosicrucians, the Freemasons, etc.—both in France and in England; he met Bulwer-Lytton, the author of the famous occult novel *Zanoni*, and he made a certain impression on Mme Blavatsky, the founder of the Theosophical Society.

Eliphas Lévi, who died in 1875, was held in great store by the following generation of French neo-occultists. The most notable among his disciples was Dr. Encausse, born in 1865, who used the pseudonym "Papus."[5] He claimed that he had acquired the initiatory ritual of that rather mysterious individual, Don Martines de Pasqually (1743–74), who founded a new esoteric order pompously entitled the Franc-Maçonnerie des Chevaliers Maçons Elus Cohen de l'Univers.[6] Papus also pretended to be the "true disciple" of Saint-Martin, the Philosophe Inconnu.[7] I cannot examine here the central thesis of Martines de Pasqually; it suffices to say that for him the goal of initiation was to reintegrate man with his lost "Adamic privileges," i.e., to recover the primeval condition of "men-gods created in the image of God." Such convictions were shared by the Philosophe Inconnu and by most of the eighteenth-century Christian *théosophes*. Indeed, for all these authors, man's original condition before the Fall was susceptible of being regained through "spiritual perfection," theurgy (i.e., evocation of angelic spirits), or alchemical operations. The countless secret societies, mystical groups, and Masonic lodges of the eighteenth century pursued, all of them, the regeneration of the fallen man. Their central symbols were the Temple of Solomon, which was to be symbolically rebuilt; the Order of Knights Templars, which was to be at least partially reconstituted; and the Grail, whose myth and hidden meaning were supposedly present in the operations of spiritual alchemy.

Papus claimed to have had access to this entire occult tradition. Accordingly, he created—his expression was "reconstituted"—the Martinist Order, through which he was willing to disclose to members the secret doctrine of Louis-Claude de Saint-Martin. But, according to the *cognoscenti*, this Order reflected almost exclusively Papus' own ideas. Nevertheless, the Martinist Order had a great success at the beginning. Among the members of its first "supreme council" were a number of well-known writers, for example, Maurice Barrès, Paul Adam, Joseph Péladan, Stanislas de Guaita, and others. At the same time, Papus aided in the foundation of other occult groups such as L'Eglise Gnostique Universelle and L'Ordre Kabbalistique de la Rose-Croix.

What is significant in this *fin de siècle* interest in the occult is the role played by French writers. Even a skeptic like Anatole France declared, in an article published in 1890, that

a certain knowledge of the occult sciences became necessary for the understanding of a great number of literary works of this period. Magic occupied a large place in the imagination of our poets and our novelists. The vertigo of the invisible seized them, the idea of the unknown haunted them, and the time returned to Apuleius and to Phlegon of Tralles.[8]

Anatole France was right. Indeed, one of the most popular novels of that epoch, *Là bas* by J.-K. Huysmans, was inspired by a contemporary black magician, the defrocked Catholic priest Abbé Boullan, and by the contest of magic between Boullan and another sorcerer, the writer Stanislas de Guaita. As a matter of fact, when Boullan died in 1893, Huysmans and other intimates of the occult group were convinced that he had been killed by de Guaita, acting as a black magician.[9] It is also worth noting that in roughly the same period a number of English writers became involved in occult practices and eagerly sought to be initiated into secret hermetic societies. I would remind you of the Order of the Golden Dawn, which counted among its members William Butler Yeats, S. L. Mathews, and Aleister Crowley.[10]

I will not examine the later history of these occult movements or the origin and development of Mme Blavatsky's Theosophical Society and other parallel groups, such as the Anthroposophical Society of Rudolf Steiner. Two observations must be made at this point, however. (1) The most erudite and devastating critique of all these so-called occult groups was presented, not by a rationalist "outside" observer, but by an author from the inner circle, duly initiated into some of the secret orders and well acquainted with their occult doctrines; furthermore, that critique was directed, not from a skeptical or positivistic perspective, but from what he called "traditional esotericism." This learned and intransigent critic was René Guénon. (2) With some exceptions, the occult movements did not attract the attention of competent historians of ideas of the times but did fascinate a great number of important writers, from

Baudelaire, Verlaine, and Rimbaud to André Breton and some of the postsurrealist authors, such as René Daumal.

I shall have more to say apropos of René Guénon and his radical critique of all the occult and pseudo-spiritualist movements of the past century. For the moment, let us consider the impact of such conceptions on European writers, and particularly the significance of their interest in the occult. Already in the eighteenth century, during the Enlightenment, and in the pre-Romantic and Romantic periods of the first part of the nineteenth century, a number of German and French authors were making free use in their writings of occult and theosophical lore. Between 1740 and 1840 a number of very popular and sometimes excellent novels and short stories came into being, signed by Goethe (*Wilhelm Meisters Wanderjahre*), Schiller (*Der Geistesseher*, 1787), Jean-Paul (*Die unsichtbare Loge*, 1793), Achim von Arnim (*Der Kronenwachter*, 1817), Novalis (*Die Lehrlinge von Sais*, 1797–98), Zacharias Werner (*Die Söhne des Thales*, 1803), Charles Nodier (*Trilby*, 1822; *Jean Sbogar*, 1818; etc.), Balzac (*Séraphita*, 1834), and others. Obviously, it is difficult to reduce all these literary works to a common denominator. However, it can be stated that their occult themes and ideology reflected a hope in a personal or collective *renovatio*—a mystical restoration of man's original dignity and powers; in sum, the literary creations reflected and prolonged the conceptions of seventeenth- and eighteenth-century theosophists and of their sources.

Quite another orientation is evident among those French authors of the second part of the nineteenth century who became attracted to the occult ideas, mythologies, and practices made popular by Eliphas Lévi, Papus, and Stanislas de Guaita. From Baudelaire and Verlaine, Lautréamont and Rimbaud, to our own contemporaries, André Breton and his disciples, all these artists utilized the occult as a powerful weapon in their rebellion against the bourgeois establishment and its ideology.[11] They reject the official contemporary religion, ethics, social mores, and aesthetics. Some of them are not only anticlerical, like most of the French intelligentsia, but anti-Christian; they refuse, in fact, all the Judeo-Christian values as well as the Greco-Roman and Renaissance ideals. They have become interested in the Gnostic and other secret groups, not only for their precious occult lore, but also because such groups have been persecuted by the Church. In the occult traditions these artists were looking for pre-Judeo-Christian and pre-Classical (pre-Greek) elements, i.e., Egyptian, Persian, Indian, or Chinese creative methods and spiritual values. They sought their aesthetic ideals in the most archaic arts, in the "primordial" revelation of beauty. Stéphane Mallarmé declared that a modern poet must go *beyond* Homer, because the decadence of Western poetry began with him. And when the interviewer asked, "But what poetry existed before Homer?" Mallarmé responded, "The Vedas!"

The writers and artists of the twentieth-century avant-garde went even further: they sought new sources of inspiration in the plastic arts of the Far East and in African and Oceanic masks and statues. André Breton's surrealism proclaimed the death of the entire Western aesthetic tradition. With other surrealists, like Eluard and Aragon, he adhered to communism; he likewise looked for poetic inspiration in different drives of the Unconscious, but also in alchemy and satanism. René Daumal taught himself Sanskrit and rediscovered Indian aesthetics; moreover, he was convinced that, through Gurdjiev, the mysterious Caucasian Master, he had discovered an initiatory tradition long forgotten in the West.[12] To conclude, from Baudelaire to André Breton, involvement with the occult represented for the French literary and artistic avant-garde one of the most efficient criticisms and rejections of the religious and cultural values of the West—efficient because it was considered to be based on historical facts.

I am stressing this aspect of the problem because, as is generally known, artistic revolutions (i.e., transmutations of aesthetic values) anticipate what will take place after one or two generations in a larger segment of society. Moreover, the writers' interest in the occult was, at least partially, contemporary with Freud's investigations of the Unconscious and with the discovery of the psychoanalytic method, which contributed considerably to the changing of European mores and modes of thought. Freud substantiated the gnoseologic values of the products of fantasy, which, until then, were considered meaningless or opaque. Once the expressions of the Unconscious became articulated in a meaning-system comparable to a nonverbal language, the immense number of imaginary universes reflected in literary creations disclosed a deeper, and secret, significance, quite independent of the artistic value of the respective works.

Esoteric Doctrines and Contemporary Scholarship

Coming now to more recent times, one is struck by a significant difference: while the nineteenth-century writers' involvement in the occult was not accompanied by a comparable curiosity on the part of historians of ideas, the reverse situation has come about in the past thirty or forty years. While there are still a number of authors who follow the line of Huysmans or André Breton, the decisive and illuminating contributions to the understanding of occult traditions have been made by historians of ideas. As a matter of fact, one can almost say that the fantastic popularity of the occult which started in the middle sixties was anticipated by a series of fundamental scientific books on esoteric doctrines and secret practices published between 1940 and 1960. Of course, we must keep in mind that two of the most famous discoveries of the century brought to light a number of documents emanating from secret or esoteric groups. I am referring to the Gnostic library of Nag Hammadi and to the manuscripts found in the Dead Sea caves, which most probably belonged to an Essene community. The publication and translation of these documents are still in progress. Nevertheless, much light has already been thrown on two problems that were extremely controversial until a generation ago.

But independently of these archeological discoveries, contemporary scholarship had produced a number of invaluable works which radically modified our understanding and appreciation of the esoteric spiritual tradition. First of all, there are the splendid monographs of Gershom Scholem on the Kabbalah and Jewish Gnosticism and mystical systems. Scholem's erudition and insight disclosed a very coherent and profound world of meaning in texts that had generally been dismissed as magic and superstition. Examples of works less well known by nonspecialist readers are the many books on, and translations of, esoteric Ismaili treatises from the Persian Islamic tradition, brought to light by Henri Corbin and his disciples.[13] Or the publications of René de Forestier on the eighteenth-century occult Freemasons; Alice Joly and Gerard van Rijnbeck on Martines de Pasqually and the secret lodges of Lyon; Antoine Faivre on eighteenth-century esotericism; and others.[14] Also, in the past thirty years we have witnessed a more correct and comprehensive appraisal of the Chinese, Indian, and Western alchemies. Until recently, alchemy was regarded either as protochemistry, i.e., an embryonic, naïve, or prescientific discipline, or as a mass of superstitious rubbish that was culturally irrelevant. The investigations of Joseph Needham and Nathan Sivin have proved the holistic structure of Chinese alchemy, that is, that it is a traditional science *sui generis*, not intelligible without its cosmologies and its ethical and, so to say, "existential" presuppositions and soteriological implications.[15] Studying Indian alchemy, I found out its organic relations with Yoga and Tantra, i.e., with specific psychomental techniques.[16] And it is significant that, in China, alchemy was intimately related to the Taoist secret practices; in India, it was a part of the Tantric Yoga; and, in the West, Greco-Egyptian and Renaissance alchemy was usually connected with Gnosticism and Hermeticism, i.e., with a secret "occult" tradition.

If I am allowed to refer to my limited personal experience, I would add that when, in 1928, as a young student, I went to study Yoga and Tantra with S. N. Dasgupta at Calcutta University, the good, competent books on these topics could be counted on one's fingers. Today there are perhaps fifty or sixty serious publications, and some of them contain editions and translations of Sanskrit and Tibetan texts supposed to be secret, that is, to circulate exclusively among the members of certain sects. (It is true, however, that such texts are almost unintelligible without the oral commentary of a master.) Moreover, while a half-century ago most of the Yogic and

Tantric texts were judged to be pure nonsense or products of obscurantist fakirs and psychopathic black magicians, contemporary Western and Indian scholarship has abundantly proved their theoretical coherence and their great psychological interest.[17] To cite another example: when, in the forties, I began studying Siberian and Central Asiatic shamanism, only two monographs on the topic existed, both in German; today there is a considerable bibliography in most of the western European languages.[18] Shamanism was, a generation ago, considered to be either a psychopathic phenomenon or a primitive healing practice and archaic type of black magic, but contemporary scholarship has convincingly demonstrated the complexity, the rigor, and the rich spiritual meaning of shamanistic initiation and practices. Such results are of consequence if we keep in mind that shamanism is the most archaic and most widely distributed occult tradition. It is needless to add that, today, Yoga, Tantra, and shamanism are very popular in the American youth culture and play a certain role in the current vogue of the occult.[19]

A most surprising result of contemporary scholarship was the discovery of the important role magic and Hermetic esotericism played, not only in the Italian Renaissance, but also in the triumph of Copernicus' new astronomy, i.e., the heliocentric theory of the solar system. In a recent book, *Giordano Bruno and the Hermetic Tradition*, Frances A. Yates has brilliantly analyzed the deep implications of the passionate interest in Hermeticism in this period. This interest discloses the Renaissance man's longing for a "primordial" revelation which could include not only Moses and Plato but also *Magia* and *Cabbala* and, first and foremost, the mysterious religions of Egypt and Persia. It reveals also a profound dissatisfaction with medieval theology and the medieval conception of man and the universe, a reaction against what we may call "provincial," that is, purely *Western* civilization, and a longing for a universalistic, transhistorical, "mythical" religion. For almost two centuries Egypt and Hermeticism, that is, Egyptian magic and esotericism, obsessed innumerable theologians and philosophers—believers as well as skeptics and crypto-atheists. If

Giordano Bruno acclaimed Copernicus' discoveries enthusiastically, it was not primarily for their scientific and philosophical
importance; it was because he thought that heliocentrism had a
profound religious and magical meaning. While he was in England,
Bruno prophesied the imminent return of the occult religion of the
ancient Egyptians as described in *Asclepios*, a famous Hermetic
text. Bruno felt superior to Copernicus, for, whereas Copernicus
understood his own theory only as a mathematician, Bruno claimed
that he could interpret the Copernican celestial diagram as a hiero-
glyph of divine mysteries.[20]

I could cite other examples, but I will conclude this review with a
brief discussion of the contemporary reevaluation of European
witchcraft. Some eighty years ago, eminent scholars such as Joseph
Hansen and Henry Charles Lea considered that the origins of Western witchcraft were definitely known: it was the Inquisition, not the
witches, that invented witchcraft. In other words, all the stories of
witches' covens, satanist practices, and orgies and crimes were
regarded as either imaginary inventions of neurotic persons or declarations obtained from the accused during the trials, especially by
means of torture. This was evidently true during the witch crazes of
the fifteenth, sixteenth, and seventeenth centuries. But we now
know that witchcraft was not invented by the Inquisition. The Inquisition merely assimilated witchcraft to heresy and consequently
proceeded to exterminate so-called witches with the same inclem-
ency it showed to heretics. That witchcraft could not have been an
invention of the Inquisition was plainly evident to any historian of
religions familar with non-European, particularly Indo-Tibetan,
materials, where many similar features appear.[21]

But the problem of the *origin* of Western witchcraft was still
unsolved. In 1921 a former Egyptologist, Margaret Murray, published *The Witch-Cult in Western Europe*, a most influential book,
which still has a great audience, especially among the young. Dr.
Murray argued that what was called witchcraft by ecclesiastical
authors represented, in fact, a pre-Christian, archaic religion of
fertility. In subsequent books the author went even further, trying to
prove the survival of the pagan cult even among the British royal

family and the highest levels of the ecclesiastical hierarchy. Understandably, Murray's theory was criticized by archeologists, historians, and folklorists alike. As a matter of fact, almost everything in her construction was wrong except for one important assumption: that there existed a pre-Christian fertility cult and that specific survivals of this pagan cult were stigmatized during the Middle Ages as witchcraft. This idea was not new, but it became popular through Murray's books. I hasten to add that neither the documents with which she chose to illustrate her hypothesis nor the method of her interpretation are convincing. Nevertheless, recent research seems to confirm at least some aspects of her thesis. The Italian historian Carlo Ginsburg has proved that a popular fertility cult, active in the province of Friule in the sixteenth and seventeenth centuries, was progressively modified under pressure of the Inquisition and ended by resembling the traditional notion of witchcraft.[22] Moreover, recent investigations of Romanian popular culture have brought to light a number of pagan survivals which clearly indicate the existence of a fertility cult and of what may be called a "white magic," comparable to some aspects of Western medieval witchcraft.[23]

Thus, to sum up, contemporary scholarship has disclosed the consistent religious meaning and the cultural function of a great number of occult practices, beliefs, and theories, recorded in many civilizations, European and non-European alike, and *at all levels of culture*, from folk rituals—such as magic and witchcraft—to the most learned and elaborate secret techniques and esoteric speculations: alchemy, Yoga, Tantrism, Gnosticism, Renaissance Hermeticism, and secret societies and Masonic lodges of the Enlightenment period.

The Most Recent "Occult Explosion"

It is difficult to determine the relation between the results of such recent scholarship and the "occult explosion" of the seventies. Perhaps only so-called white-magic lodges, flourishing now in England, reflect the influence of Murray's theory. There seems to be no relation between scientific research carried out on the history of astrology—of rather modest proportions, to be sure—and the amazing popularity of this most ancient occult discipline. Even if we had more time at our disposal, we could not present a complete picture of the contemporary craze for astrology in both the United States and Europe. Suffice it to say that at least 5 million Americans plan their lives according to astrological predictions, and some 1,200 of the 1,750 daily newspapers in this country publish horoscopes.

> There is enough business to keep ten thousand full-time and one hundred seventy-five thousand part-time astrologers at work. An estimated 40 million Americans have turned the zodiac business into a $200-million-a-year enterprise. Currently there are several computers engaged in the casting and interpretation of horoscopes. One of these prints out a ten-thousand-word horoscope in minutes for twenty dollars. Another provides twenty-four-hour-a-day horoscopes to about two thousand campuses across the country. A third computer is located in Grand Central Station, putting out about five hundred horoscopes a day.[24]

Of course, astrology, the hope that one can know the future, has always been popular with the rich and powerful—with kings, princes, popes, etc.—particularly from the Renaissance on. One may add that the belief in the determination of destiny by the position of the planets illustrates, in the last analysis, another defeat of Christianity. Indeed, the Christian Fathers fiercely attacked the astrological fatalism dominant during the last centuries of the Roman Empire. "We are above Fate," wrote Tatian; "the Sun and the Moon are made for us!"[25] In spite of this theology of human freedom, astrology has never been extirpated in the Christian world. But never in the past did it reach the proportions and prestige it enjoys in our times. What a fantastic progress from the first monthly periodical, which appeared in London in August 1791, to the many thousands of astrological magazines published today all over the Western world. The history of the vertiginous fame and prestige of astrology in modern societies makes fascinating reading. The glory of Evangeline Adams, who arrived in New York in 1899 and soon became "America's female Nostradamus," is only a modest example. Mary Pickford and Enrico Caruso brought all the cinema and opera stars to her, and it was rumored that the financier J. Pierpont Morgan "never made an important move on Wall Street" without consulting Evangeline Adams. Other astrologers became famous in the '30s, for instance Thomas Menes, who was said to have "an unbroken record for making predictions that came true."[26] Though most of his predictions proved erroneous, his prestige did not suffer. It is needless to remind you of Hitler's interest in astrology. You may read in H. R. Trevor-Roper's book, *The Last Days of Hitler*, how, in the middle of April 1945, Hitler and Goebbels again consulted the horoscope which predicted a major victory for late April and peace in August. However, Hitler took his life on April 30, and the German army surrendered on May 7. Finally, we may recall the innumerable astrological programs that have appeared on television, in spite of the interdiction voted by the National Association of Broadcasters in March 1952, and such best-sellers as *A Gift of Prophesy* by Ruth Montgomery, which sold more than 260,000 copies as a hard-cover and 2,800,000 as a paperback.

What can be the explanation of such fantastic success? Recently, a number of French sociologists and psychologists published a book, *Le Retour des astrologues* (1971), in which they present and analyze the results of an investigation based on data gathered by the French Institute of Public Opinion.[27] I will not summarize the social characteristics of believers in astrology, classified by sex, occupation, age, and the size of the localities where the data were gathered. I will quote only some of the conclusions: Edgar Morin, for instance, interprets the appeal of astrology among youth today "as stemming from the cultural crisis of bourgeois society." He thinks that, in the youth culture, "astrology is also part of a new gnosis which has a revolutionary conception of a new age, the Age of Aquarius." What is highly relevant is the fact that the greatest interest in astrology "is not to be found in the countryside, among farmers or among the lower ranges of the occupational structure, but rather in the most densely populated urban centers and among white-collar workers."[28]

The French authors did not insist on the parareligious function of astrology, yet the discovery that your life is related to astral phenomena does confer a new meaning on your existence. You are no longer merely the anonymous individual described by Heidegger and Sartre, a stranger thrown into an absurd and meaningless world, condemned to be free, as Sartre used to say, with a freedom confined to your situation and conditioned by your historical moment. Rather, the horoscope reveals to you a new dignity: it shows how intimately you are related to the entire universe. It is true that your life is determined by the movements of the stars, but at least this determinant has an incomparable grandeur. Although, in the last analysis, a puppet pulled by invisible ropes and strings, you are nevertheless a part of the heavenly world. Besides, this cosmic predetermination of your existence constitutes a mystery: it means that the universe moves on according to a preestablished plan; that human life and history itself follow a pattern and advance progressively toward a goal. This ultimate goal is secret or beyond human understanding; but at least it gives meaning to a cosmos regarded by most scientists as the result of blind hazard, and it gives sense to the human existence declared by Sarte to be *de trop*. This parareligious dimension of astrology is even considered superior to the existing religions, because it does not imply any of the difficult theological problems: the existence of a personal or transpersonal God, the enigma of Creation, the origin of evil, and so on. Following the instructions of your horoscope, you feel in harmony with the universe and do not have to bother with hard, tragic, or insoluble problems. At the same time, you admit, consciously or unconsciously, that a grand, though incomprehensible, cosmic drama displays itself and that you are a part of it; accordingly, you are not *de trop*.

Such self-promotions to a respectable status are achieved with a greater intensity in most of the contemporary so-called magic and occult movements. I will not discuss some of the widely publicized Satanist lodges, such as that of Anton LaVey, high priest and founder of the Church of Satan in San Francisco. Readers interested in this type of aggressive revolt against the theistic interpretation of the world may read LaVey's own book, *The Satanic Bible*.[29] Also, although for different reasons, I will not examine certain occult schools, like the one founded by Gurdjiev and interpreted by Ouspensky, René Daumal, and Louis Pauwels. Moreover, there are a few recent Californian groups reputed to practice ceremonial magic and witchcraft, but the information available is scarce and suspect. However, what has been called the "occult explosion" has attained such proportions that it is easy to select examples to illustrate the general orientation of these new secret, magicoreligious cults.[30] Thus, in Robert Ellwood's book, *Religious and Spiritual Groups in Modern America*, one can find data about such cults as the Builders of the Adytum, the Church of Light, the Church of All World, or the Feraferia.[31] We learn that the Builders of the Adytum, founded by Paul Foster Case (1884–1954), focus their spiritual life upon the Hermetic and Kabbalistic traditions. "The temple is brilliant with beautiful luminous paintings of the Tarot cards around the walls, and the altar is rich with the black and white pillars of Solomon and the Kabbalistic Tree."[32] The Church of Light was founded in 1932 by Elbert Benjamine (1882–1951), who claimed that in 1909 he "undertook a mysterious journey during which he was inducted as a member of a council of three" who manage the affairs of an arcane order in their world. The Church of Light has fifty degrees of initiation, "culminating in the Soul Degree, in which one must demonstrate there has been specific realization of higher states of consciousness."[33] A rather unusual sect, even judged by the standards of the contemporary understanding of the occult, is the Church of All Worlds, founded in 1961 by two students at Westminster College in Missouri after reading *Stranger in a Strange Land*, by the noted science-fiction writer Robert A. Heinlein. The members greet each other with the phrase "Thou art God." In fact, each human being is God and therefore has God's responsibility: "whether the world ravages itself to death, or the lovely goddess [i.e., the whole biosphere of earth] comes to consciousness on this planet, is up to us."[34]

Finally, I will cite the neopagan movement Feraferia, centered in Pasadena, California. It is probably among the most recent, having been incorporated by its founder, Frederick M. Adams, on 2 August 1967. It has only 22 initiates and about 100 members. The group celebrates seasonal festivals and practices nudism. "Feraferia holds that religious life should be a part of sensitive interaction with nature and one's own erotic awareness."[35] Their central symbol is the Greek goddess Kore, Demeter's daughter. The initiation ritual achieves an identification with nature and with Kore, the divine Maiden, and the initiates strive to recover a primeval horticultural paradise. "Feraferia sees itself as a precursor of a future culture in which the feminine archetype will again be restored—in Magic Maiden form—to religious centrality, and in which mankind will recover a sense of reverence in his dealings with nature and life."[36]

The Hope for *Renovatio*

Many of these cults and sects will undergo radical transformations or will decline or disappear, probably to be replaced by other groups. In any event, they are representative of the contemporary youth culture and express the craze for the occult with more vigor and clarity than do older organizations, like the Theosophical Society or Anthroposophy. They all exhibit a number of specific traits. First and foremost, all of these secret and initiatory groups proclaim their dissatisfaction with the Christian church, whether Roman Catholic or Protestant. In more general terms, one can speak of a revolt against any traditional Western religious establishment. This rebellion does not imply a theological or philosophical critique of specific dogmas and ecclesiastical institutions but rather a more sweeping dissatisfaction. As a matter of fact, most members of the new cults are almost completely ignorant of their own religious heritage, but what they have seen, heard, or read about Christianity has disappointed them. There are segments of the young generation that expected other spiritual instruction from their churches besides social ethics. Many of those who tried to partake actively in the life of the church were looking for sacramental experiences and especially for instruction in what they call, vaguely, "gnosis" and "mysticism." Of course, they were disappointed. In the past fifty years, all the Christian denominations have decided that the most urgent task of the church is to be vigorously relevant on the social plane. The only Western Christian tradition which conserved a powerful sacramental liturgy, the Roman Catholic Church, is now trying drastically to simplify it. Moreover, "gnosis" and gnostic speculations were, from the very beginning, persecuted and condemned by ecclesiastical authorities. As for the mystics and mystical experiences, the Western churches barely tolerated them. One can say that only Eastern Orthodox Christianity has elaborated and conserved a rich liturgical tradition and has encouraged both gnostic speculation and mystical experience.

I hasten to add that such dissatisfaction with the Christian tradition does not explain the growing interest in the occult which started in the sixties and paved the way for the occult explosion of the seventies. It is true that in some cases the provocative promotion of witchcraft and gnosticism had also an anticlerical intention: one can decipher in such boastful proclamations a sort of revenge taken by the victims of ecclesiastic persecution. But such cases are sporadic. What is more general is a rejection of Christian tradition in the name of a supposedly broader and more efficient method for achieving an individual and, by the same stroke, a collective *renovatio*.[37] Even when these ideas are naïvely or even ludicrously expressed, there is always the tacit conviction that a way out of the chaos and meaninglessness of modern life exists and that this way out implies an *initiation* into, and consequently the revelation of, old and venerable secrets. It is primarily the attraction of a *personal* initiation that explains the craze for the occult. As is well known, Christianity rejected the mystery-religion type of secret initiation.[38] The Christian "mystery" was open to all; it was "proclaimed upon the housetops," and Gnostics were persecuted because of their secret rituals of initiation. In the contemporary occult explosion, the "initiation"—however the participant may understand this term—has a capital function: it confers a new status on the adept; he feels that he is somehow "elected," singled out from the anonymous and lonely crowd. Moreover, in most of the occult circles, initiation also has a superpersonal function, for every new adept is supposed to contribute to the *renovatio* of the world.

Such a hope is evident in the effort to rediscover the sacrality of nature. The importance of ceremonial nudity and ritual intercourse must not be interpreted as merely lustful inclinations. The recent sexual revolution has made obsolete such types of pretense and masquerade. Rather, the purpose of ritual nudity and orgiastic practices is to recapture the sacramental value of sexuality. One can speak of the unconscious nostalgia for a fabulous, paradisiacal existence, free from inhibitions and taboos. It is significant to note that in most occult circles the notion of freedom is part of a system, involving the ideas of cosmic *renovatio*, religious universalism (meaning, especially, the rediscovery of the Oriental traditions), and spiritual growth through initiation, a spiritual growth that continues, of course, in the afterlife. In sum, all the recent occult groups imply, consciously or unconsciously, what I would call an optimistic evaluation of the human mode of being.

Another Look at Esotericism: René Guénon

This naïve optimism can be—and, in fact, has been—criticized from many perspectives. However, more significant than the rationalistic views, like, for instance, the one that sees in the occult revival a form of "pop" religion, is the radical rejection by the foremost representative of modern esotericism, René Guénon. Guénon, born in 1886 in a Catholic family, became interested in the occult as a young man; but, after being initiated into many Parisian secret societies, he abandoned them and decided to follow the Oriental tradition. He became a Muslim in 1912 and in 1930 went to Egypt, where he spent the rest of his life, dying in 1951.[39] Now, if he could witness the contemporary occult explosion, René Guénon would have written a considerably more devastating book than his *Le Théosophisme: Histoire d'une pseudo-religion* (1921). In this learned and brilliantly written book, Guénon debunked all the so-called occult or esoteric groups, from Mme Blavatsky's Theosophical Society and Papus to the many neospiritualist or pseudo-Rosicrucian lodges. Considering himself a *real* initiate and speaking in the name of the *veritable* esoteric tradition, Guénon denied not only the authenticity of modern Western so-called occultism but also the ability of any Western individual to contact a valid esoteric organization. For Guénon, only one branch of Freemasonry had conserved some parts of a traditional system; but he added that the majority of the Lodge's members were unaware of this heritage. Consequently, Guénon never ceased to contend in his many books and articles that only in the East are true esoteric traditions still alive. Moreover, he pointed out that any endeavor to practice any of the occult arts represents, for contemporary man, a serious mental and even physical risk.

It is obviously impossible here to summarize Guénon's own doctrine.[40] For our purposes, it suffices to say that he definitely rejects the general optimism and hope in a personal and cosmic *renovatio* which seem to characterize the occult revival. Already in his books *Orient et Occident* and *La Crise du monde moderne*, published in 1924 and 1927, Guénon proclaimed the irremediable decadence of the Western world and announced its end. Using the terms of the Indian tradition, he stated that we are rapidly approaching the final phase of the Kali-yuga, the end of a cosmic cycle. For Guénon, nothing can be done to change or even to retard this process. Consequently, there is no hope for a cosmic or social *renovatio*. A new cycle will begin only after the total destruction of the present one. As for the individual, Guénon believed that the possibility of contacting one of the initiatory centers surviving in the East exists in principle but that the chances of doing so are very limited.

What is even more important—and in radical contradiction with the ideas implicit in recent occult movements—Guénon denied the privileged status of the human personality. He literally states that man

> represents only a transitory and contingent manifestation of true being. . . . Human individuality . . . ought not to

have a privileged place "out of series" in the indefinite hierarchy of states of total being; there it occupies a rank no more important than that of other states.[41]

During his life, René Guénon was a rather unpopular author. He had fanatical admirers, but their number was limited. Only since his death, and especially in the past ten to twelve years, have his books been reprinted and translated, making his ideas more widely known. This phenomenon is rather curious, because, as I have said, Guénon presents a pessimistic view of the world and announces its imminent catastrophic end. It is true that some of his disciples do not insist too much on the inevitable end of the actual historical cycle but try to develop his insights concerning the function of the esoteric tradition in specific cultures.[42] I may also add that most of his disciples are converts to Islam or students of the Indo-Tibetan tradition.

Thus we witness a rather paradoxical situation: on the one hand, an occult explosion, a sort of "pop" religion, characteristic especially of the American youth culture, which proclaims the great renewal of the post-Aquarian age; and, on the other hand, a more modest but progressively growing discovery and acceptance of traditional esotericism, as reformulated, for example, by René Guénon, which rejects the optimistic hope of cosmic and historic renewal without the preliminary catastrophic dissolution of the modern world. These two tendencies are radically opposed. There are some signs of an effort to soften the pessimistic outlook of Guénonian doctrines, but it is too early to judge its results.

A historian of religions must resist the temptation to predict what will happen in the near future—in our case, to predict how these two opposite understandings of the occult tradition will develop. We might at least try to compare the contemporary situation with that of the nineteenth and the beginning of the twentieth centuries, when, as we have seen, writers and artists also displayed a great interest in the occult. But today the artistic and literary imagination is too complex to permit such a sweeping generalization. The literature of *fantasy* and the fantastic, especially in science fiction, is much in demand, but we still do not know its intimate relationship with the different occult traditions. The underground vogue of Hesse's *Journey to the East* (1951) in the fifties anticipated the occult revival of the late sixties. But who will interpret for us the amazing success of *Rosemary's Baby* and *2001?* I am merely asking the question.

5 Some Observations on European Witchcraft

As a historian of religions, I cannot fail to be impressed by the amazing popularity of witchcraft in modern Western culture and its subcultures. However, in the present essay I will not discuss this craze because the contemporary interest in witchcraft is only part and parcel of a larger trend, namely, the vogue of the occult and the esoteric—from astrology and pseudospiritualist movements to Hermetism, alchemy, Zen, Yoga, Tantrism, and other Oriental gnoses and techniques. But no less fascinating for a historian of religions are recent attempts at interpretation and controversies relating to the origin and growth of Western witchcraft, particularly the reexaminations of the sixteenth- and seventeenth-century witch craze. One has only to quote the works of Etienne Delcambre, H. R. Trevor-Roper, J. B. Russell, or Keith Thomas to realize the importance of such problems in contemporary historiography.[1] I shall utilize some of these works, but I shall not discuss their findings and conclusions or the methodological presuppositions of the authors. Rather, I shall limit my presentation to two highly controversial problems: (1) the "origins" of Western witchcraft,

This paper was first presented as the John Nuveen Lecture, given in May 1974 at the University of Chicago. A revised and expanded version was published in *History of Religions* 14 (1975): 149–72.

that is, the problem of its possible relation to pre-Christian beliefs and rituals; and (2) the so-called witches' orgies, which, from the moment witchcraft was assimilated to a heresy, were at the center of the charges brought against it.

Some eighty years ago, the problem of the origins of Western witchcraft was considered definitely solved. The learned German archivist Joseph Hansen brought out his *Zauberwahn, Inquisition und Hexenprozess* and began the publication of the records of the trials, and the no less learned American historian Henry Charles Lea published his *History of the Inquisition in the Middle Ages* and was collecting that mass of sources which was posthumously published under the title *Materials toward a History of Witchcraft*.[2] In the words of Hansen, "The epidemic persecution of magicians and witches is a product of medieval theology, ecclesiastical organization, and the magic trials conducted by the papacy and the Inquisition. These, under the influence of scholastic demonology, were conducted like heresy trials."[3] Lea likewise concluded that the Inquisition, and not the witches, invented witchcraft. Accordingly, this learned author asserted that witchcraft came into being only in the mid-fourteenth century.[4]

This opinion, reflecting the liberalism, rationalism, and anti-clericalism of the epoch and buttressed with a great number of documents, was considered, until the early 1920s, the only convincing explanation of the rise and fall of European witchcraft. Of course there were some opponents, such as Montague Summers among the more recent ones, who did not doubt the actual intervention of the Devil in the making of witches.[5] Consequently, he did not question the reality of any of the activities that witches were supposed to engage in: flights to secret meetings, adoration of Satan, infanticide, cannibalism, orgies, and so on. This ultraconservative view was shared, not only by some Catholic apologists, but also by occultists and a number of writers; it was also rather popular among the *amateurs* of the Black Mass and other Luciferian entertainments. In sum, the liberal-rationalist interpretation denied the historic existence of witches on account of the supernatural elements implied in witchcraft; the ultraconservative interpretation, on the contrary, accepted the Inquisition's charges as valid because its proponents took for granted the reality of the Devil.

The Historiography of Witchcraft and History of Religions

I do not intend to summarize here the results of the investigations of the past half-century. It suffices to say that, as work progressed, the phenomenon of witchcraft appeared more complex and consequently more difficult to explain by a single factor. Gradually it became evident that witchcraft cannot be satisfactorily understood without the help of other disciplines, such as folklore, ethnology, sociology, psychology, and history of religions. The materials at the disposition of historians of religion are especially apt for situating witchcraft in its proper context. For instance, even a rapid perusal of the Indian and Tibetan documents will convince an unprejudiced reader that European witchcraft cannot be the creation of religious or political persecution or be a demonic sect devoted to Satan and the promotion of evil. As a matter of fact, all the features associated with European witches are—with the exception of Satan and the Sabbath—claimed also by Indo-Tibetan yogis and magicians. They too are supposed to fly through the air, render themselves invisible, kill at a distance, master demons and ghosts, and so on. Moreover, some of these eccentric Indian sectarians boast that they break all the religious taboos and social rules: that they practice human sacrifice, cannibalism, and all manner of orgies, including incestuous intercourse, and that they eat excrement, nauseating animals, and devour human corpses.[6] In other words, they proudly claim all the crimes and horrible ceremonies cited *ad nauseam* in the western European witch trials.

Unfortunately, the few attempts to investigate the phenomenon of European witchcraft in the perspective of history of religions have been hopelessly inadequate. One such attempt had an unexpected success and became popular, especially among the dilettantes. I refer to Margaret Murray's book *The Witch-Cult in West-*

ern Europe, published in 1921 by Oxford University Press. For more than a half-century, Dr. Murray's theory was the most influential one, and her article on witchcraft in the *Encyclopaedia Britannica* was, until recently, reprinted in many successive editions. From the very beginning, a number of scholars pointed out Murray's many factual errors and methodological failings.[7] But the impact of *The Witch-Cult in Western Europe* was such that, as late as 1962, an English historian, Elliot Rose, devoted almost an entire book, *A Razor for a Goat*, to a close analysis and a devastating, though humorous, criticism of her theory. That theory, aptly summarized by Rose, is that

> the witch was essentially a member of a cult-organization, which was not in revolt against Christianity, but a wholly independent and older religion, in fact, the paganism of pre-Christian Western Europe surviving for centuries after a nominal conversion. Its worship was directed to a two-faced, horned god, identifiable with Janus or Dianus (who is fully described in the early chapters of *The Golden Bough*) and with the Celtic Cernunnos. Inquisitors in their ignorance and bigotry confused this deity with the Church's Satan, but his claims in fact were hardly less respectable than Jehovah's and locally had priority. Indeed the cult was the real popular religion of England and several neighboring countries throughout the Middle Ages. Christianity was a mere official veneer, adopted from policy, to which rulers enforced an outward conformity. Even rulers who did so, however, could not really afford to suppress the witch-cult (or, as Dr. Murray preferred to call it, Dianism). For its practices, far from being malign or antisocial, were generally considered necessary for the well-being of the community, as they had been in the days of open paganism; and for this reason they were secretly encouraged down to the time of the Reformation, by the highest persons in the state and precisely those who were publicly committed to abhorrence of the horned god and all his works. We are told that the cult, which seems to have been monotheistic, had an elaborate organization based on the coven of thirteen, which ran through all classes of society and included kings and their ministers, and even nominally, Christian prelates.[8]

As I have said, historians have pointed out the countless and appalling errors that discredit Murray's reconstruction of European witchcraft. The historian of religions can only add that her use of comparative materials and, in general, the methods of *Religionswissenschaft* has been unfortunate. However, at least one of her critics, J. B. Russell, recognizes that Murray's book has the merit of emphasizing the persistence of pagan folk practices and beliefs centuries after the introduction of Christianity.[9] As a matter of fact, many scholars, from Jakob Grimm to Otto Höfler, have repeatedly stressed the survival of pre-Christian religious beliefs and rituals, especially in western and central Europe. But the central point in Murray's thesis was that the Inquisitors viciously misinterpreted an archaic fertility cult as adoration of Satan. Now it is a well-known fact that, from the eighth century on, popular sorcery and superstition were progressively equated with witchcraft, and witchcraft with heresy.[10] But it is difficult to understand how Murray's *fertility cult* could have developed into a secret society pursuing exclusively *destructive* goals; for in fact the medieval witches were renowned for being able to cause droughts, hail, epidemics, sterility, and, in the last analysis, death. It is true that, invariably, the witches—as well as the heretics—were accused of orgiastic practices; but according to their own declarations, not always obtained by torture, the children born from such orgies were sacrificed and devoured at their secret meetings. In other words, the witch orgies could not be truly classified among the orgiastic fertility cults.

The Case of the *Benandanti*

Murray's thesis is based in large measure on English materials. Now, granted the survival of the pre-Christian fertility cult in England until medieval times, I do not know how such a self-contradictory disfiguration can be explained in light of the documentary evidence available there. Yet a similar process of development seems to have taken place in the Italian province of Friule in the sixteenth and seventeenth centuries, and this gives us valuable comparative evidence. Thanks to the researches of Carlo

Ginzburg, we know now that an Italian popular cult was progressively modified under pressure of the Inquisition and ended by resembling the traditional witchcraft.[11] I am referring to the cult of the so-called *benandanti* ("those who are traveling," "vagabonds"), attested for the first time in a document of 21 March 1575. On that day the *vicario generale* and the Inquisitor of the provinces of Aquileia and Concordia were first told that in certain villages there were wizards who called themselves *benandanti* and declared themselves "good" wizards because they fought against sorcerers (*stregoni*). The investigations of the first *benandanti* brought out the following facts: They met in secret, at night, four times a year (i.e., the four ember weeks); they reached their meeting place riding on hares, cats, or other animals; the assembly did not present any of the well-known "satanic" traits of the witch covens: there was no abjuration of the faith, no vituperation of the sacraments or the Cross, no homage to the Devil. The central ritual is rather enigmatic. The *benandanti*, provided with fennel branches, fought the sorcerers (*strighe* and *stregoni*), who were armed with broomlike reeds. The *benandanti* claimed that they opposed the witches' evil deeds and cured their victims of their spells. If the *benandanti* were victorious in the combats of the four ember weeks, then the crops of the year would be abundant; if not, there would be scarcity and famine.[12]

Further investigations brought to light some details concerning the recruitment of the *benandanti* and the pattern of their nocturnal assemblies. They claimed that they were requested to join the company by an "angel from heaven" and were initiated into the secret group when they were between twenty and twenty-eight years old. The company was organized in military fashion under a captain, and the company gathered together when they heard the captain beating a drum. The members were bound by an oath of secrecy,[13] and at their meetings sometimes as many as 5,000 *benandanti* were present, some from the same region but most of them unknown to one another. They had a flag of gilded white ermine, while the sorcerers' flag was yellow, with four devils depicted on it. All the *benandanti* had this trait in common: they were born "with the shirt," that is, enveloped in a caul.[14]

When the Inquisition—following their stereotyped notion of the witches' Sabbath—asked whether the "angel" promised them delicious food, women, and other salacious entertainments, the defendants proudly denied such insinuations. Only wizards (*stregoni*), they declared, danced and made merry at their meetings. The most enigmatic element of the *benandanti* is their "voyage" to the place of their assemblies. They claimed that they went *in spirito* while they slept. Before the "voyage," they fell into a state of great prostration, an almost cataleptic lethargy, during which their soul was able to leave the body. The *benandanti* did not use any ointments to prepare for their "voyage," which, though accomplished *in spirito*, was, for them, real.

In 1581 two *benandanti* were sentenced as heretics to six months in prison and to abjure their errors.[15] More trials took place in the following sixty years, and we shall see their consequences. For the moment let us try to reconstruct, on the basis of the documents of the epoch, the structure of this popular secret cult. Obviously, the central rite of the *benandanti* consisted of a ceremonial battle against the sorcerers in order to assure the abundance of the harvest, the vineyards, and "all the fruits of the earth."[16] The fact that this battle was fought on the four critical nights of the agricultural calendar leaves no doubt about its purpose. It is probable that this combat between *benandanti* and *stregoni* prolonged an archaic ritual scenario of competitions and contests between two opposing groups, designed to stimulate the creative forces of nature and regenerate human society as well.[17] The ceremonial combat was only superficially Christianized, although the *benandanti* claimed that they fought for the Cross and "for the faith in Christ."[18] Nor were the *stregoni* accused of the familiar theological crimes; they were guilty only of destroying the crops and of casting spells on children.[19] Only in 1634 (after 850 trials and denunciations to the Inquisition of Aquileia and Concordia) do we come across the first accusation of *stregoni* for performing the traditional diabolic Sabbath. As a matter of fact, the charges of witchcraft attested to in northern Italy do not speak of adoration of the Devil but of the cult of Diana.[20]

However, as a consequence of numerous trials, the *benandanti* began to conform to the demonological model that was persistently pressed on them by the Inquisition. We do not hear any more of the central fertility rite beyond a certain moment. After 1600 the *benandanti* conceded that they practiced only the cure of sorcerers' victims. Such an avowal was not without danger, for the Inquisition considered the ability to treat evil spells as an obvious proof of witchcraft.[21] As time passed, the *benandanti* not only became more conscious of their importance; they multiplied their denunciations of those persons supposedly known by them to be witches. In spite of this heightened antagonism, however, the *benandanti* were unconsciously drawn nearer the *strighe* and *stregoni*. In 1618 a woman *benandante* admitted that she had gone to a nocturnal Sabbath presided over by the Devil, adding, however, that she had done so in order to obtain from him the power to heal.[22]

Finally, in 1634, after fifty years of Inquisitorial trials, the *benandanti* acknowledged their identity with the witches (*strighe* and *stregoni*).[23] One defendant confessed that he anointed his naked body with a special ointment and went to the Sabbath, where he saw many witches celebrating, dancing, and having indiscriminate sexual intercourse; but he did state that the *benandanti* did not take part in the orgy. A few years later a *benandante* acknowledged that he was bound by a pact with the Devil, that he had abjured Christ and the Christian faith, and, finally, that he had killed three children.[24] Further trials brought out the inevitable elements of the by now classic image of the witches' Sabbath: the *benandanti* conceded that they went to the sorcerers' ball and that they paid homage to the Devil and kissed his hindparts. One of the most dramatic confessions took place in 1644. The accused man meticulously described the Devil and told how he had given him his soul. Further, he acknowledged that he had killed four children with evil spells. But when the prisoner was alone in his cell with the episcopal vicar, he declared that his entire confession had been a lie and that he was neither *benandante* nor *stregone*. The judges agreed that the prisoner "confesses everything which is suggested to him." We do not know what the verdict would have been, for the prisoner hanged himself in his cell. As a matter of fact, this was the last important trial of the *benandanti*.[25]

This example does not substantiate Murray's entire thesis, for there is no indication of the "two-faced, horned god" or of "elaborate organizations based on the coven of thirteen." Moreover, the *benandanti* attended their meetings in *ekstasis*, that is, in their sleep. Nevertheless, we do have here a well-documented case of the *processus* through which a popular and archaic secret cult of fertility is transformed into a merely magical, or even black-magical, practice under pressure of the Inquisition.

A noteworthy parallel to the *benandanti* may be seen in reports of the trial of an eighty-six-year-old Lithuanian, Thiess, who was accused of lycanthropy. The trial took place in Jürgensburg in 1691, and an account was published by H. van Bruiningk.[26] Otto Höfler has the merit of having attracted attention to this exceptional document, reproducing the essential sections in an appendix to his *Kultische Geheimbünde der Germanen*.[27] The aged Thiess acknowledged before his judges that he was a werewolf (*Wahrwolff*) and that, as such, he fought the Devil. Three times a year, in the nights of Saint Lucie before Christmas, of Pentecost, and of Saint John, he and his companions went on foot, transformed into wolves, to "the end of the sea," that is, hell. There they fought the Devil and the wizards, pursuing them like dogs. (On one such occasion, a long time earlier, Thiess fought with a certain wizard, Skeistan, and had his nose broken by a blow from a broom handle.) Thiess explained to the judges that the werewolves transformed themselves into wolves and descended into hell in order to bring back to earth the goods stolen by wizards, namely, cattle, wheat, and other fruits of the earth. If they did not act in time, the effects would be like those of the preceding year, when they had found the door of hell barricaded, and, because they could not take back the wheat and other grains, the crops were disastrous.

At death, declared Thiess, the souls of the werewolves go to heaven, while the wizards are taken by the Devil. The werewolves hate the Devil; they are the "dogs of God." But for their active intervention, the Devil would make the earth waste. Not only do the Lithuanian werewolves thus combat the Devil and the wizards for the sake of the crops, but the German and Russian werewolves do likewise, though they go down to other hells. When the judges tried to convince Thiess that the werewolves had a pact with the Devil, the old man vigorously protested; and to the parson—who had been called in, in the hope that he could succeed in making Thiess confess his sins—he shouted that his own deeds were more beneficial than the priest's. Until the end, Thiess refused to repent, and he was condemned to ten lashes for superstition and idolatry.

Van Bruiningk also quotes a notice from C. Peucer's *Commentarius de praecipius generibus divinationum* . . . .[28] In the course of a feast in Riga, a young man fainted, and someone present recognized him as a werewolf. The following day the young man related that he had fought a witch who wandered about in the form of a butterfly (in fact, comments Peucer, the werewolves boast that they drive away the witches). Carlo Ginzburg rightly compares the *benandanti* and the Lithuanian werewolves with the shamans, who descend ecstatically to the underworld in order to save their community.[29] On the other hand, one must keep in mind the belief, general in northern Europe, that the dead warriors and the gods fight against the demonic forces.[30]

Romanian Parallels: The *Strigoi* and the "Troop of Diana"

I will turn now to another area of study, unfortunately neglected by Western scholarship, namely, the Romanian folkloric traditions. Here we are confronted with an archaic popular culture which developed under a less rigid ecclesiastical control than was common in central or western Europe. Furthermore, the Romanian church, like all other eastern European Greek Orthodox churches, did not possess an institution analogous to the Inquisition; consequently, though heresies were not unknown, there was no systematic and massive witch persecution. What is even more important, Romanian is a Romance language which, during the Middle Ages, was not influenced by ecclesiastical and Scholastic Latin. That is to say, Romanian represents a direct development of the vulgar Latin spoken in the province of Dacia in the first centuries of our era. This linguistic archaism is of great help in understanding European witchcraft.

I will confine my analysis to two terms of decisive importance for our problem: *striga*, the Latin word for "witch," and "Diana," the Roman goddess who, in western Europe, became the chief of the witches. In Romanian the vocable *striga* became *strigoi*, meaning "witch," either as a living witch or a dead one (in that case, a vampire). The living *strigoi* are born with the caul; when they reach maturity, they put it on and become invisible. They are reported to possess supernatural powers; for instance, they can enter houses with locked doors or play unharmed with wolves and bears. They carry out all the evil doings characteristic of witches: they bring epidemics on men and cattle, "bind" or disfigure men, provoke droughts by "binding" the rain, take milk from cows, and, most especially, cast evil spells.[31] The *strigoi* can transform themselves into dogs, cats, wolves, horses, pigs, toads, and other animals.[32] They are supposed to go out on specific nights, especially the nights of Saint George and Saint Andrew; and when they come back home, they turn somersaults three times and recover their human form. Their souls leave their bodies and ride on horses, brooms, or barrels. The *strigoi* gather together outside the villages in a particular field or "at the end of the world, where does not grow grass." Once there, they take human form *and begin to fight among themselves*, using clubs, axes, scythes, and other instruments. They fight all night long, but in the end they cry and become reconciled with one another. They return to their houses exhausted, pale, without knowing what happened to them, and fall into a deep sleep.[33] Unfortunately, nothing is known about the significance or the object of these nocturnal battles. One is reminded of the *benandanti* and also of the *Wilde Heer*, the troop of the dead so common in central and western Europe. But the *benandanti* were fighting precisely against the *striga*, while the Romanian *strigoi* fight among themselves, their battles always being concluded with a general weeping and reconciliation. As for the analogy to the *Wilde Heer*, it lacks the most characteristic trait: the terrific noise that terrorizes the village.[34] In any case, the Romanian witches illustrate the authenticity of a pre-Christian scenario founded on oneiric voyages and ecstatic ritual combat, a pattern attested to in many other European regions.

Let us now turn to the second Latin word which played an important role in Romanian folk beliefs: "Diana." The history of this goddess in the ancient province of Dacia (the Carpatho-Danubian regions inhabited now by Romanians) may throw unexpected light on the development of European witchcraft in general. Indeed, among the Western peoples speaking Romance languages—Italian, French, Spanish, Portuguese—medieval references to beliefs and rituals related to Diana may, in the main, be suspected of reflecting the opinion of learned monks familiar with Latin written sources. No such suspicion can arise with regard to the history of Diana among Romanians. The very name of the goddess became in Romanian *zîna* (< *dziana*), meaning "fairy." Moreover, there is another word deriving from the same root: *zînatec*, meaning "one who is thoughtless, scatterbrained, or crazy," that is, "taken" or possessed by Diana or by the fairies.[35] It is very probable that the name Diana replaced the local name of an autochthonous Thraco-Getic goddess.[36] In any case, the archaism of the rituals and beliefs related to the Romanian Diana is unquestionable.

Now, the *zîne*, the fairies who show in their own name their descent from Diana, display a rather ambivalent character. They can be cruel, and for this reason it is safer not to pronounce their name. One refers to them as "The Holy Ones," "The Munificent Ones," "The Rosalia," or simply "They" (*iele*). The fairies are immortal but look like beautiful girls, playful and fascinating. They are clothed in white, with their breasts nude, and are invisible during the day. They are provided with wings, and they fly through the air, especially at night. The fairies love to sing and dance, and on the fields where they have danced the grass looks as if burnt by a fire. They strike with illness persons who see them dancing or who fail to respect certain interdictions. Among the diseases which they cause, the most common are psychomental affections, rheumatism, hemiplegia, epilepsy, cholera, and the plague.[37]

The *Căluşari*—Cathartic Dancers

All these maladies are successfully cured by the choreographic and cathartic ritual of a group of dancers, who constitute a sort of secret society (*Männerbund*) called *căluşari*, a name derived from the Romanian term for "horse," *cal* (< Lat. *caballus*).[38] Now, surprisingly enough, the patroness of this secret cathartic society is the "Queen of the Fairies" (*Doamna Zînelor*)—the Romanian metamorphosis of Diana. She is also called Irodiada (= Herodiada) or Arada, both names famous among western European witches.[39] We cannot here enter into details concerning the selection, instruction, and initiation by an elder leader of a group of seven, nine, or eleven young men. It suffices to say that the instruction is carried out in forests or lonely places and consists mainly in learning a great number of dances, especially acrobatic ones. The *căluşari* are armed with clubs and swords, and they carry a wooden horse's head and a "flag," on which they swear to respect the *căluşari*'s customs and rules, to be like brothers to one another, to observe chastity for the coming nine (or twelve or fourteen) days, not to divulge to any outsider what they will see or hear, and to obey the leader. After the oath-taking, the "flag," with medicinal plants tied to its tip, is hoisted, and the *căluşari* are forbidden to speak, for fear, they say, of being made sick by the *zîne*.[40]

The central and specific attribute of the *căluşari* is their acrobatic-choreographic skill, especially their ability to create the impression of flying in the air. It is obvious that springing, leaping, jumping, and bounding indicate the galloping of the horse and, *at the same time*, the flying and the dancing of the fairies (*zîne*). As a matter of fact, some of those who are supposed to have been made sick by the fairies begin to jump and shout "like the *căluşari*," and "seem not to touch the earth." The relations between *căluşari* and *zîne* are paradoxically ambivalent: the dancers ask for and count on the protection of Herodiada, but they also risk becoming the victims of her troop of attendants, the fairies. The *căluşari* imitate the flying of the *zîne*, but at the same time they emphasize their solidarity with the horse, a masculine and "heroic" symbol par excellence. These ambivalent relations are manifest also in their patterns of behavior and their activities. For approximately two weeks the *căluşari* visit all the villages and hamlets in the neighborhood, accompanied by two or three fiddlers, dancing and playing and at times trying to cure the victims of the fairies. It is believed that during the same period, that is, from the third week after Easter until around Whitsunday, the *zîne* are flying, singing, and dancing, especially by night; one can hear their bells and also the drums and other musical instruments, for the fairies have at their service a number of fiddlers and bagpipers and even a flag-bearer.[41] The most effective protection against the fairies is garlic and mugwort, that is, the same magico-medicinal plants that are in the bag tied atop the flag of the *căluşari*. The *căluşari* chew as much garlic as they can stand, and, in the course of a cure, the leader spits garlic on the patient's face.[42]

The military, para-*Männerbund* elements of the *căluşari* are evident: the flag, the sword, the wooden horse's head, the clubs. Moreover, if two groups of *căluşari* meet each other, they engage in a violent fight. When the group returns to the village, the final dramatization is called the "war." Their flag is solidly fixed in the ground, and one *căluşar* climbs the pole and shouts: "War, dear ones, war!"[43] Although the oath-taking is made in the name of God, the mythico-ritual scenario enacted by the *căluşari* has nothing in common with Christianity. We can assume that in early times the ecclesiastical authorities fought against them with some violence, for a number of archaic traits, attested in the seventeenth century, have disappeared. Even as late as the end of the nineteenth century the *căluşari* were, in some regions, excluded from communion for three years.[44] But finally the Church decided to tolerate them.

The Merging of the Opposites: *Sântoaderi* and *Zîne*

The origin of the *căluşari* is obscure, and I will not endeavor to discuss it now.[45] But I will cite an illuminating parallel to the ambivalent relationship between the *zîne* and the *căluşari*. In Romanian popular beliefs an important role is played by a group of seven or nine mythological figures called *Sântoaderi* (taking their names from Saint Theodore). They are described as young men with long feet and hooves, having manes that are covered by their cloaks. They visit the villages, singing and beating their drums, appearing suddenly and then mysteriously disappearing. One hears the metallic sound of their heavily shod feet. They dance on the bodies of their victims, or they bind them with chains, thus provoking rheumatic pains. Young girls are particularly afraid of the *Sântoaderi* and do not dare to venture out of the house during the three nights before Shrove Tuesday. Most of these elements seem to be remnants of an old *Männerbund*, with its characteristic violence aimed at terrorizing women.[46]

However, on the night of Saint Theodore, the unmarried girls go to the forest or climb a hill, and around a kindled fire they dance and sing in chorus: "Theodore, Saint Theodore, make the girls' manes grow like the mare's tail. I give you bread and salt, you give me lots of hair; I give you bread and nuts, you bring me sweet lips!" They sing and dance until dawn and then return to the village, gathering all sorts of herbs and flowers on the way. What they have gathered is then boiled in water, and they wash their hair with this water. They then believe that they will marry soon. Thus the patron saint of the horselike *Sântoaderi*, the terror of women and particularly of young girls, is invoked by them to make their hair as beautiful as the horse's mane and to hasten their marriage.

In sum, there is a curious rapport between the *zîne* and the *Sântoaderi*: both groups travel by night on a specific date, singing, dancing, and accompanied by fiddlers. Both bring specific diseases to punish those who break certain interdictions; both are mysteriously related to magical and medicinal plants (in the case of the fairies, a few specific herbs serve to keep them afar; and other plants, collected in the name of Saint Theodore, hasten the girls' marriages). Moreover, twenty-four days after Easter there is a feast when the fairies meet the *Sântoaderi* and play with them, finally offering each of them a bouquet of a particular flower (*Melites melissophylum*, a species of mint or balm).[47] This feast *emphasizes the desire to bring together two classes of supernatural beings who represent, for human society, different but equally malicious forces.*

Now, these "mythological" horse-men, *Sântoaderi*, cannot be identified with the initiatic and cathartic group of *călușari*, although the latter are also literally designated as "horse-men." But the folkloric scenario which brings together two classes of mythological beings—the fairies and the *Sântoaderi*—finds a striking parallel in the mythico-ritual scenario of the *căluşari*: a para-*Männerbund* secret association, renowned for its powers to cure the victims of the *zîne*, is nevertheless under the protection of "Diana," the Queen of the Fairies (*Doamna Zînelor*). Although the *căluşari* use apotropaic imagery and substances (i.e., the horse, the medicinal plants) to defend themselves against the fairies (*zîne*), their cathartic and therapeutic techniques are based mainly on a particular choreography which imitates the mode of being and the behavior of the fairies. In the last analysis, the scenario actualized by the *căluşari* consistently implies *the merging of opposite, though complementary, magico-religious ideas and techniques*. The amazing persistence of this archaic scenario finds its most probable explanation in the fact that the antagonistic "principles" which are pacified and brought together—sickness and death, health and fertility—were personified in one of the most inspiring expressions of the primeval feminine-masculine dyad, the fairies and the horse-riding cathartic heroes.

This archaic, pre-Christian scenario survived, with inevitable modifications and loss of some original elements, only in Romania. Needless to add, the origin and development of such a mythico-ritual pattern does not explain the origin of Western witchcraft. But the Romanian documents do contribute significantly to our understanding of the process which produced witchcraft and black magic in western Europe. First, there now can be no doubt concerning the continuity of some important pagan rituals and beliefs, mainly related to fertility and health. Second, such mythico-ritual scenarios involved a fight between two groups of opposite, though complementary, forces, personified in mythological (and late, folkloric) figures, ritually impersonated by young men and women (cf. *benandanti,: striga, căluşari*). Third, the ceremonial fight was in some cases followed by reconciliation between the antithetical groups. Fourth, this ritual bipartition of the collectivity implied a certain ambivalence, for one of the two opposing groups always impersonated the negative aspects of the antagonism, expressing the process of cosmic life and fertility; moreover, at a certain moment in history or on certain occasions, the impersonation of the negative principle could be interpreted as a manifestation of *evil*.[48] This seems to have happened in the case of the Romanian *strigoi* and, to a certain extent, to the *zîne*, the fairies who correspond to "Diana's troop," as well. Under pressure of the Inquisition, a similar modification took place with the *benandanti*. In the West this process was considerably more complex, thanks to the early identification of any pre-Christian mythico-ritual survival with satanic practices and, finally, with heresy. Of course, I do not mean to say that sorcery and black magic did not exist, everywhere in Europe, from time immemorial. But these practices were always restricted to a few individuals. What medieval authors designated as witchcraft, and what became the witch crazes of the fourteenth, sixteenth, and seventeenth centuries, had its roots in some archaic mythico-ritual scenarios comparable with those surviving among the Italian *benandanti* and in Romanian folk culture. In times of religious and social crisis, under economic or ecclesiastical pressure, such popular survivals could have received, either spontaneously or as a result of the Inquisition trials, a new orientation—specifically, toward black magic.

Lucerna Extincta

I come now to the second standard accusation made against the witches: their orgiastic practices. One of the first such testimonies was obtained by Stephen of Bourbon, Inquisitor in southern France from 1235. A woman told him the following story:

> She had a mistress who frequently led her to an underground place where a crowd of men and women assembled with torches and candles. They gathered round a large vessel full of water into which a rod had been thrust (a fertility rite?). The master then called upon Lucifer to come to them. Thereupon a cat of hideous appearance decended the rod into the room. Dipping his tail into the water, he brought it out wet and

used it as an aspergill. Then the lights were all extinguished and each person seized his neighbor in promiscuous embrace.[49]

With few variants, this description of the witches' Sabbath is abundantly recorded in the following centuries. The specific elements are the meeting in an underground place, the evocation and appearance of Satan, and the extinguishing of the lights, followed by indiscriminate sexual intercourse. Such monotony becomes suddenly significant when we find out that, from the beginning of the eleventh century, *exactly* the same accusation was made against different Reformist movements imputed to be heresies. Thus in 1022, at Orléans, a group of Reformists were charged with holding sex orgies at night in underground caves or abandoned buildings. According to the prosecution, the devotees chanted the names of demons; and when one evil spirit appeared, the lights were put out and each member of the group seized whoever lay closest, whether mother, sister, or nun. "The children conceived at the orgies were burned eight days after birth . . . and their ashes were made into a substance that was used in a blasphemous parody of Christian communion."[50]

Such incriminations became a cliché and were repeated apropos of every individual or group accused of heresy. A report from 1175 indicates that the heretics of Verona congregated in a subterranean hall and, after hearing a blasphemous sermon, put out the lights and held an orgy.[51] Exactly the same charges were imputed in the eleventh century to the Patarenes, the German heretics, and the Cathari.[52] In the thirteenth century the Brethren of the Free Spirit from the Rhineland, the Apostolici from North Italy, the Luciferians who appeared in Germany from 1227, and the Bohemian Adamites in the fourteenth and fifteenth centuries were reported to hold sexual orgies in subterranean places.[53] According to Konrad of Marburg, the first papal Inquisitor in Germany, the sectarians (of the thirteenth century) used to gather in a secret place; the Devil appeared in the form of an animal, and, after songs and a short liturgy, the lights were extinguished and a bisexual orgy occurred.[54] In the fourteenth and fifteenth centuries the Waldensians and the

Cathari were even more radically assimilated to witches, or vice versa. The Cathari were reported to meet during the night, and, after hearing sermons and receiving heretical sacraments, they feasted and drank, and finally the lights were extinguished.[55] The same accusation was lodged against the Brethren of the Free Spirit[56] and even against the Fraticelli (i.e., the Reformist Franciscans): the latter "held their orgy after extinguishing the lights and killed the children born as a result, grinding their bones into a sacramental powder."[57]

Now we must recall that similar indictments—sexual orgies, incest, cannibalism—were made by the pagans against Christians. And the Christian writers, from Aristides and Justin Martyr to Tertullian and Minucius Felix, repeatedly tried to refute the clichés that became so popular after the trial of Orléans, namely, extinction of light, orgies, incest, and ritual infanticide followed by cannibalistic communion, using the child's flesh and blood. In the third century Christian authors began charging the pagans with perverse and cannibalistic rites. But their real campaign was directed against the Christian heretics. Already in 150 Justin Martyr accused the heretics of sex orgies, incest, and anthropophagy "with the lights extinguished" (*aposbennuntes tous luchnous*).[58] The same formula was applied by Clement of Alexandria against the Carpocratians, Montanists, and Gnostics. Augustine claimed that *lucerna extincta* and sex orgies were practiced by the Manichaeans. Analogous accusations were repeated, between the seventh and ninth centuries, against the Messalians, Paulicians, and Bogomils.[59]

No scholar will accept such charges, indiscriminately brought against medieval witches and Reformist or "heretical" movements as well as the early Christians and the Gnostic and sectarian groups. On the other hand, it seems difficult to admit that ceremonial meetings and sexual orgies following the ritual extinction of lights can be explained away as a pure invention, consciously or unconsciously used against a despised religious minority. It is true that such expressions as *in loco subterraneo* or *lucerna extincta* became powerful and popular clichés. But if a cliché does not prove the existence of the action it incriminates, neither does it prove its nonexistence. Such clichés as *in loco subterraneo* or *lucerna extincta* belong to imaginary universes, and we are now beginning to acknowledge the importance of that mysterious *sur-réalité* revealed by any imaginary universe. Thus one finds the formula "extinction of lamps" in the description of some orgiastic practices of Central Asia. And among the Shaktic and Tantric circles of the Himalayan region, especially at Garhwāl, the ritual orgy was called *coli-marg* because each man received as partner in the rite the woman whose breast cloth he had drawn by lot (*coli* = breast cloth). Also, the *rāsamaṇḍalī*, literally "circles of play," of the Vallabhācāryas often degenerate into orgies.[60] The authenticity of some of these accounts has been contested. However, from what we know of the Russian sectarians and also of the sect of Innocentists of Bessarabia, such orgies were not at all improbable.[61]

Moreover, ritual orgies—in some cases preceded by the extinction of lights—are attested among populations as different as the Kurds, the Tibetans, the Eskimos, the Malgaches, the Ngadju Dyaks, and the Australians. The incentives are manifold, but generally such ritual orgies are carried out in order to avert a cosmic or social crisis—drought, epidemic, strange meteorological phenomena (e.g., the aurora australis)—or in order to lend magico-religious support to some propitious event (a marriage, the birth of a child, etc.) by releasing and heightening the dormant powers of sexuality.[62] Over against a dangerous crisis as well as an auspicious event, indiscriminate and excessive sexual intercourse plunges the collectivity into the fabulous epoch of the beginnings. This is clearly evident in the practice of periodical orgies at the end of the year or at specific sacred intervals. As a matter of fact, it is this type of ritual orgy, undoubtedly the most archaic, which discloses the original function of promiscuous collective intercourse. Such rituals reactualize the primordial moment of the Creation or the beatific stage of the beginnings, when neither sexual taboos nor moral and social rules yet existed. Perhaps the most impressive illustrations of this concept are to be found among the Ngadju Dyaks and some Australian tribes.

Ritual Orgies and the Nostalgia for the "Beginnings"

For the Ngadju Dyaks the end of the year signifies the end of an era and also the end of a world. The ceremonies clearly indicate that there is a return to precosmic time, the time of the sacred totality. In fact, during this period, sacred par excellence, all the population of the village returns to the primeval (i.e., precosmogonic) age. Rules and interdictions are suspended, since the world has ceased to exist. While waiting for a new creation, the community lives near the godhead, more exactly, lives *in* the total primeval godhead. The orgy takes place in accordance with the divine commandments, and those who participate in it recover in themselves the total godhead. As Schärer puts it, "there is no question of disorder (even if it may appear so to us), but of another order." [63]

In the Dyak case, one can interpret the periodical ritual orgy as the longing to rejoin the perfect primordial totality that existed before the Creation. But there are also other forms of this nostalgia for the beginnings. The Central Australian Aranda tribes periodically celebrate the creative works their mythical ancestors performed while they were roaming about the land. That marvelous epoch is for the Arandas tantamount to a paradisiacal age. Not only did the different animals allow themselves to be easily captured, and water and fruits were in abundance, but the ancestors were free from the multitude of inhibitions and frustrations that inevitably obstruct all human beings who live together in organized communities. [64] This primeval paradise still haunts the Arandas. One can interpret the brief intervals of ritual orgies, when all interdictions are suspended, as ephemeral returns to the freedom and beatitude enjoyed by the ancestors. [65]

Such a religious nostalgia for the beatific times of the mythical beginnings seems to be ineradicable. The Adamites, sectarian Bohemians of the fourteenth and fifteenth centuries, strived to recapture the state of Adam's innocence—their mythical ancestor and ours. Accordingly, they went naked and practiced free love, men and women living together in a perfect and uninhibited sexual promiscuity. [66] In the early fourteenth century, Lazarus, a monk from Mount Athos and a former Bogomil, founded his own sect, proclaiming nudism as the means par excellence for recovering the stage prior to the Fall.[67] Another sect was created by an itinerant preacher, Theodosius. He not only requested ritual nudity but encouraged his followers to indulge in orgiastic excesses in order to receive the grace of repentance.[68] A similar justification was claimed in the nineteenth and twentieth centuries by the Russian sect of the Innocentists: they lived practically naked in underground caves and engaged exclusively in indiscriminate sexual intercourse, hoping to be redeemed by the enormity of their sins.[69]

One hesitates to range such wild orgiastics among Christians or even among Christian sectarians. Because of the Judeo-Christian *demonization* of sexuality, any type of orgy was considered satanic and consequently a sacrilege, deserving the harshest punishment. But, as is well known, the sacrality of sexual life could not be radically extirpated, either in Judaism or in Christianity. For ritual nudity and ceremonial free intercourse were not only powerful magico-religious forces; they also expressed the nostalgia for a beatific human existence, which, in this Judeo-Christian context, corresponded to the paradisiacal state before the Fall. From the religious perspective, the tragic catastrophe of the first parents implies, among other calamities, the interdiction of nudity and the loss of spontaneous sexual innocence. Accordingly, endeavors to recapture the lost powers and beatitudes were, directly or indirectly, consciously or unconsciously, accompanied by a radical modification of sexual mores.

It is difficult if not impossible to distinguish between the *real* and the *imaginary* elements in the witches' testimonies with regard to their secret "orgies." A great number of depositions are obviously the result of ecclesiastical inquests, whether Catholic or Lutheran and Calvinist. This insistence on the old cliché proves that the theologians were well aware of the magico-religious powers of sexuality. Such powers were able to transform Christians into sacrilegious heretics and ultimately into dangerous, demonic beings. Denouncing them as Devil-worshipers was only a convenient routine. The decisive fact was that, imaginary or not, the witches' orgies, like those of the heretics, could endanger the social and theological institutions; indeed, they released nostalgias, hopes, and desires aiming at a mode of being different from the typical Christian existence. If we keep in mind the fact that rural populations are in general only moderately interested in sex, it seems evident that such sexual ceremonial excesses pursued other objectives than simple lustful gratification. It was not mere carnal desire that incited country women to become witches. It was the obscure hope that, by breaking the sexual taboos and partaking of "demonic" orgies, they somehow could transmute their own condition. In the last analysis, it was the magico-religious forces of the prohibited sexual practices that tempted one to become a witch, even if such sacrilegious adventures were performed in an imaginary universe. As a matter of fact, most of the witches allude to the lack of pleasure in their intercourse with the Devil. As we read their testimonies, it sounds more like a harsh initiatory trial than a *partie de plaisir*. This painful character of the witches' orgies was well known, and not only among those who eventually became suspected of witchcraft. Of course, the prosecutors could have forced the accused to admit having had sexual intercourse with the Devil. But there are also cases of spontaneous testimonies of young girls, abundantly and vividly describing their "initiatory" rape by the Devil—until medical examination proved that they were virgins.[70]

To conclude: the real or imaginary orgiastic practices of European witches disclose a certain religious pattern. First and foremost, the sexual orgies reveal a radical protest against contemporary religious and social situations—a revolt incited and nourished by the hope of recovering a lost beatific perfection, namely, that of the fabulous "beginnings," a beatitude that haunts the imagination, particularly during catastrophic crises. Second, the so-called satanic elements of the witch orgies may have been practically nonexistent but forcibly imposed by the trials; ultimately, the satanist clichés became the principal indictment in the denunciations made during the witch crazes. But it is also possible that practices described as satanic were really consummated; in such cases, they expressed a rebellion against Christian institutions that failed to "save" man, and especially against the decadence of the Church and the corruption of the ecclesiastical hierarchy. Moreover, we must also keep in mind the irresistible attraction toward evil among certain types of personality. Third, whatever may have been the causes, the important fact is that the orgiastic practices witness to a religious nostalgia, a strong desire to return to an archaic phase of culture—the dreamlike time of the fabulous "beginnings."

Something similar is happening in our day, mainly in the youth culture. To begin with, there is a total dissatisfaction with existing institutions—religious, ethical, social, political. Such a rupture with the past is existentially ambivalent: on the one hand, it expresses itself through aggressiveness and rebellion against all kinds of rules and dogmas and the so-called establishment, all of which are unconsciously likened to the persecution and tyranny of some modern kind of Inquisition; on the other hand, the rejection of modern social structures and moral values, which implies a rejection of civilization and, in the last analysis, of history, has a religious meaning, although this religious dimension is seldom recognized as such. Indeed, one notices among some sections of the youth culture the rediscovery of "cosmic religion" and the sacramental dimension of human existence; elements pointing in this direction are, for instance, communion with nature, ritual nudity, uninhibited sexual spontaneity, the will to live exclusively in the present, and so on. Moreover, the interest in the occult, so characteristic of the youth culture, also indicates the desire to reanimate the old beliefs and religious ideas that are persecuted, or are at least frowned upon, by the Christian churches (astrology, magic, gnosis, alchemy, orgiastic practices) and to discover and cultivate non-Christian methods of salvation (Yoga, Tantra, Zen, etc.).

All these have to do with the same fundamental drive: to go beyond one's parents' and grandparents' world of meanings and to recover the lost significance and beatitude of the "beginnings" and thereby the hope of discovering a new and *creative* mode of existing in the world.

6 Spirit Light and Seed

In an article written in 1957, I discussed a number of experiences, mythologies, and speculations related to "mystical light."[1] My main design was to establish a morphology that would facilitate a relevant comparative analysis. Essentially, the essay had a methodological intention, namely, to show that only by comparing similar religious phenomena can one simultaneously grasp their general structure and their particular, specific meanings. I have chosen to investigate the experiences and ideologies of "mystical light" precisely because of their extensive distribution in space and time. Indeed, we have at our disposal a large number of examples from different religions, not only archaic and Oriental but from the three monotheistic traditions, Judaism, Christianity, and Islam. What is even more significant, there also exists a rich documentation relating to spontaneous or "natural" experiences of inner light, that is, experiences undergone by individuals without any ascetic or mystical preparation and apparently even without religious interests.

I do not intend to summarize here the results of my investigation. As could be expected, the morphological similarities and dif-

This paper was first published in *History of Religions* 11, no. 1 (August 1971): 1–30. I have added, in the notes, some recent bibliographical information.

ferences among such experiences point to distinct, but comparable, religious or theological meanings. If I may quote from my concluding remarks, all types of light-experiences have this factor in common:

> they bring a man out of his profane universe or historical situation, and project him into a universe different in quality, an entirely different world, transcendent and holy. The structure of this holy and transcendent Universe varies according to a man's culture and religion. Nevertheless they share this element in common: the Universe revealed through a meeting with the Light contrasts with the profane Universe— or transcends it—by the fact that it is spiritual in essence, in other words only accessible to those for whom the Spirit exists. The experience of Light radically changes the ontological condition of the subject by opening him to the world of the Spirit. In the course of human history there have been a thousand different ways of conceiving or valorizing the world of the Spirit. That is evident. How could it have been otherwise? For all conceptualization is irremediably linked with language, and consequently with culture and history. One can say that the meaning of the supernatural Light is directly conveyed to the soul of the man who experiences it—and yet this meaning can only come fully to his consciousness clothed in a preexistent ideology. Here lies the paradox: the meaning of the Light is, on the one hand, ultimately a personal discovery; and, on the other hand, each man discovers what he was spiritually and culturally prepared to discover. Yet there remains this fact which seems to us fundamental: whatever will be the subsequent ideological integration, a meeting with the Light produces a break in the subject's existence, revealing to him— or making clearer than before—the world of the Spirit, of holiness and of freedom; in brief, existence as a divine creation, or the world sanctified by the presence of God.[2]

The different light-experiences discussed in my essay, with the exception of the few spontaneous ones, were constantly valorized in their traditional contexts. In sum, a certain light-experience was considered a religious experience because, in the already existing mythological or theological systems, light was considered an expression of divinity, spirit, or sanctified life. Certainly, we do not find universally a well-articulated theology or metaphysics of the divine light, comparable, for instance, with the Indian, Iranian, or Gnostic systems. But one cannot doubt the "experiential" character of the majority of mythologies, theologies, and gnoses based on the equivalence: light–divinity–spirit–life. In other words, after reviewing, even only in part, the rich and impressive documentation relating to the experience of "mystical light," it is difficult to presume that, in the religions and sects where light was supremely valorized, such experiences were not the source, the presupposition, or the confirmation of the respective light-theology.

In the present article I intend to make a more elaborate analysis by limiting the discussion to documents implying a doctrine in which light is an expression of both divinity and the human soul (or spirit) and, at the same time, of divine creativity and thus of cosmic and human life; in the last analysis, I shall be dealing with a series of identifications and homologizations beginning with godhead and ending with *semen virile*. I shall therefore limit the investigation to Indian, Iranian, and Gnostic documents, by and large. However, I shall also discuss the example of a South American tribe for the insights it offers into such types of religious experience.

Antarjyotiḥ and the Solar Seed

The connaturality of godhead, sun, light, spirit (*ātman*) and the creative energy at work on all cosmic levels seems to have been grasped already in the Vedic age.[3] In *Rig Veda* X. 121. 1, Prajāpati the Creator is presented as Hiraṇyagarbha, "the Golden Embryo," that is, the solar seed.[4] The Brāhmaṇas explicitly consider the *semen virile* a solar epiphany. "When the human father thus emits him as seed into the womb, it is really the Sun that emits him as seed into the womb,"[5] for "Light is the progenitive power."[6] But in the *Brihadāraṇyaka Upaniṣad* the *semen virile* is the vehicle only of the Immortal (i.e., *ātman*-Brahman): "He who is present in[7] the semen, whom the semen does not know, whose body (vehicle) the semen is, that is your self (*ātman*), the inner controller, the Immortal."[8] However, the *Chāndogya Upaniṣad* (III. 17. 7) relates the "primeval seed" to the light, the "highest light," and ultimately to the sun.[9]

As is well known, the sun as a progenitor is an extremely widespread conception. In many American myths and folktales the notion of virginity is expressed by vocables meaning "not sunstruck."[10] In ancient Egypt, life flows as light from the sun or as semen from the phallus of a creative god.[11] We shall encounter similar, though rather complex, speculations while discussing some more-recent Near Eastern documents.

Coming back to the Upanishads, I need not recall the passages, already discussed in my *Méphistophélès et l' Androgyne* (pp. 27–30; English translation, pp. 26–28), where light is declared identical with being (*ātman*-Brahman) and immortality. It suffices to emphasize the fact that, for the Indian mind, there is only one possible concrete (experiential) verification of what may be called the "realization of the Self" (*ātman*), and this is the experience of the "inner light" (*antarjyotiḥ*; cf. *Brih. Up.* IV. 3. 7). This "realization" is sudden, "like the lightning which flashes forth" (*Kena Up.* IV. 4). The instantaneous, luminous comprehension of being is at the same time a revelation of the metaphysical truth; "In lightning—truth" (*Kauṣītaki Brāhmaṇa Up.* IV. 2). Likewise, varicolored lights—called in the *Śvetāśvatara Up.* (II. 11) "preliminary forms of Brahman"—are experienced by the ascetics and the yogins during their meditations (*M & A*, pp. 30—33; English translation, pp. 28–31).

Understandably, the gods are "more radiant than the Sun and Moon." Every manifestation of Brahmā is revealed by "the light that rises and the glory that shines."[12] Furthermore, the birth or illumination of the great saviors and sages is announced by a profusion of supernatural light. Thus, in the night in which Mahāvīra was born, "there was one great divine, godly lustre."[13] But it is particularly in Buddhist texts and iconography that light-epiphanies abound. I have already quoted a number of examples (*M & A*, pp. 36 ff.; English translation, pp. 33 ff.): at the birth of a Buddha five

cosmic lights shine, and every Buddha can light the whole universe
with the tuft of hair which grows between his eyebrows. Gautama
declares that at the end of a discourse he "becomes a flame." When
Buddha is in *samādhi*, "a ray called the 'Ornament of the Light of
Gnosis,' proceeding from the opening in the cranial protuberance
(*uṣṇīṣa*), plays above his head."[14] Examples can easily be multiplied.[15] Immediately after attaining *Nirvāṇa*, flames start to emerge
from Gavāmpati's body, and he is self-cremated.[16] Likewise,
Ananda ignites in spontaneous combustion and attains *Nirvāṇa*.[17]
Of course, we are dealing with a pan-Indian conception. From the
heads of famous Hindu yogis and contemplatives a flame always
rises, and from their bodies a fiery energy radiates.[18]

Denying the existence of *ātman* as an ultimate, irreducible
spiritual entity, the Buddhists explained the experience of an inner
self-luminosity by the proper nature of pure thought. As is stated in
Aṅguttara-nikāya 1. 10: "Luminous is this thought, but sometimes
it is stained by adventitious passions." Elaborating on this passage,
some Hīnayāna schools assert that thought is originally and naturally luminous (*cittaṃ prabhāsvaram*) but can be defiled (*kliṣṭa*) by
passions (*kleśa*) or released from passions (*vipramukta*). However,
the passions do not belong to the original nature of thought and so
are qualified as adventitious (*āgantuka*).[19] For certain Yogācāra
authors the "luminous thought" is identified with the "embryo of
the Tathāgata" (*Tathāgatagarbha*). Thus a *sūtra* quoted in the
Laṅkāvatāra describes the *Tathāgatagarbha* as "naturally luminous, pure, hidden in the bodies of all beings."[20] Discussing the
nature of the Self (*ātman*), *Mahaparinirvāṇa Sūtra* states that "*ātman* is the *Tathāgatagarbha*. All beings possess the Nature of
Buddha: this is *ātman*. But, from the beginning, this *ātman* is
always covered by innumerable passions (*kleśa*); for this reason the
beings do not succeed in seeing it."[21]

One can say that, according to this theory, man's original nature
is a self-luminous spiritual being (= thought, *ātman*) identical with
an embryo of a Buddha. The nature of "reality," thought, and
Buddhahood is light. One may compare the conception of the embryo of the Tathāgata, buried in all bodies, with the old Indian
series of homologies: godhead–spirit–light–seed.

Mongols and Tibetans: The Seminal Light

The consubstantiality godhead–spirit (soul)–light–*semen virile* is vouched for also in Tibet and among the Mongols.[22] According to legend, Genghis Khan's ancestor was born from a divine being who descended into the tent through the smoke-hole, appearing like a luminous trail, and whose light penetrated the mother's body.[23] With regard to the birth of Shenrab, the founder and patron of Bon religion, there exist two parallel legends; one of them, closely imitating Sākyamuni's nativity, tells how a ray of white light, looking like an arrow, entered the crown of his father's skull, while a red ray, resembling a spindle, sank into the mother's head. In another, more ancient, version, it is Shenrab himself who descended from the heavenly palace in the form of five colors (i.e., like a rainbow); he metamorphosed into a bird, perched on the head of his mother-to-be; and two rays, one white and the other red, emerged from his genitals and penetrated, through the skull, the body of the woman.[24] According to the Tibetans, at the time of procreation the soul of the child enters the mother's head through the *sutura frontalis* (*brāhmarandhra*), and it is through the same orifice that the soul leaves the body at the moment of death.[25] The operation carried out by the lama in order to hurry the soul's departure through the *brāhmarandhra* is called "to shoot an arrow through the roof-hole"; this arrow is luminous, and it is imagined as a shooting star.[26]

The Tibetan myths summarized in *M & A* (pp. 47 ff.; English translation, pp. 41 ff.) explain the origin of the universe and man from a white light or a primordial being. According to a parallel tradition, in the beginning men were infused by their own interior light and were asexual. The sun and moon did not exist as yet. But when the sexual instinct awoke, the genital organs appeared; and, while the light was extinguished in men, the sun and moon appeared in the firmament.[27]

Light and Semen in Tantrism

It is difficult to decide whether these conceptions reflect Indian (or archaic Indo-Iranian) traditions or are influenced by late Iranian, that is, Manichaean, theories.[28] The idea of a consubstantiality of (divine) spirit, light, and *semen virile* is certainly Indo-Iranian and may be even more archaic. On the other hand, there is at least one instance where Manichaean influences are plausible, namely, Candrakirti's interpretation of the secret Tantric rite *maithuna*. As is well known, in Buddhist Tantrism the ritual intercourse with the "girl" (*mudrā, yoginī*) must not end in a seminal emission (*boddhicittaṃ notsṛjet*).[29] Tucci pointed out as early as 1935 the importance of Candrakirti's commentary and Ts'on k'a pa's glosses on *Guhyasamāja Tantra*.[30] Following a long tradition,[31] Candrakirti interprets the Tathāgatas or *skandhas* as being mere luminous elements; but he specifies that "all Tathāgatas are five lights," that is, that they are variously colored. Candrakirti enjoins that during the meditation the disciple must imagine the Buddha situated in a dazzling light. Ts'on k'a pa explains that the absolute truth—the immediate intuition (*nirvikalpa*)—is the mystical knowledge of this light. Commenting upon the mystic union of the Buddha with the corresponding *śakti*, Candrakirti and Ts'on k'a pa affirm that the *boddhicitta* (literally, "thought of enlightenment") is the drop, *bindu*, which flows from the top of the head and fills the two sexual organs with a flash of fivefold light: "During the time of the union [with the *śakti*] one must meditate upon the *vajra* (= *membrum virile*) and the *padma* (= womb) as being filled in the interior with the fivefold light, white, etc."[32] For Tucci, "the importance of the luminous elements in the process of cosmic emanations as that of mystic salvation" shows a striking analogy with the five luminous elements which play a central role in Manichaean cosmology and soteriology.[33]

Like so many other Buddhist and Hindu Tantras, the *Guhyasamāja* abundantly illustrates the multifarious and sometimes unexpected revalorizations of an archaic ritual and a traditional religious ideology. Sexual intercourse and erotic symbolism have been documented in Indian religious life since Vedic times.[34] The *maithuna* as a sacramental act, aiming at identification of the human couple with their divine models (Śiva and Śakti, Buddha and his *prajña*),[35] is a prerequisite in left-hand Hindu Tantrism and in many Vajrayāna schools. But what is striking in *Guhyasamāja*

Tantra and its commentaries is the effort to "experience" the five mystical lights during a sexual union, which is a ceremonial "play" (*līlā*), since no seminal emission should take place (*boddhicittaṃ notsṛjet*). As we have seen (p. 96), such varicolored lights are experienced by ascetics and contemplatives during their yogic meditations. According to the Indo-Tibetan tradition, similar lights confront the soul immediately after death, in the state of *bardo*.[36] The "experiential" character of such ecstatic photisms cannot be doubted. One can quote innumerable analogous examples from documents describing spontaneous or drug-induced inner-light experiences.[37] Thus, we must stress again the "experiential" reality of the mystic lights: they correspond to authentic psychic phenomena; that is, they are not willfully "imagined" or rationally invented and classified in order to construct a cosmological or anthropological "system."

In regard to the Tantric injunction *boddhicittaṃ notsṛjet*, we may recall the Manichaean interdiction against emitting the semen and rendering the woman pregnant. The meaning and the function of the seminal retention are undoubtedly different in Manichaeism and Tantrism. However, in Manichaeism, too, the *semen virile* is identified with the cosmic and divine light (see p. 107, below).

"*Kuṇḍagolaka*": The Play and the Fool

But the secret Tantric ritual also presents other parallels with some Gnostic ceremonies. In the Hindu Tantric tradition, *maithuna* does not necessarily imply the withholding of the *semen virile*.[38] We are, however, very poorly informed with regard to these complicated sexual ceremonies pursuing specific religious experiences. Thus, for instance, in his voluminous treatise *Tantrāloka*, the great eleventh-century Hindu author, Abhinavagupta, describes *maithuna* as a ritual aimed at obtaining *ānandaviśrānti*, "rest in bliss." During the ceremonial union, "one attains the state of complete repose (*viśrāntidharma*), and all phenomenal objects are merged into one's own self."[39] But as the authors of the most recent work on Abhinavagupta remark:

The verses actually dealing with intercourse are deliberately couched in obscure and symbolic terms,[40] so that it is very difficult to understand precisely what is meant. . . . The passages concerning the actual ejaculation of semen are the most obscure of all. It is clear from p. 89 and elsewhere that the face of the *śakti* is the most important *cakra* of all, and it would seem, though we are not certain if we have understood the passages correctly (e.g., p. 88), that the man ejaculates in the mouth of the woman. From the many quotations that Jayaratha cites, it is obvious that there existed a very elaborate and serious literature on this subject, unfortunately lost today. In explaining the difficult verse on p. 91 (verse 128) Jayaratha explains that the semen should be passed back and forth from the mouth of the woman to the mouth of the man, and finally poured into a consecrated vessel. Several verses from "the *āgamas*" are quoted in support. . . . Abhinava himself discusses various forms of ejaculation, all supported by ancient authorities.[41]

Analyzing the same passages from *Tantrāloka*, Tucci points out that the *kuṇḍagolaka*—that is, the mixture of semen and *śonita*, the female secretions—is collected in the consecrated vessel. The commentary of Jayaratha indicates that *kuṇḍagolaka* can be eaten.[42] As Tucci writes:

That such a thing can be eaten is confirmed also by some practices followed in the higher initiations of the rÑin ma pa in Tibet, which show great contamination with Tantric Śaiva literature. The reason is that *kuṇḍagolaka* is homologous with *cit*, or *citta*, the Consciousness *ab initio* which is present within us, though imprisoned in time and space; the ceremony— provided it is not performed for mere pleasure but for acquiring a full understanding of what its experience means—reproduces the process of the creation (*visarga*) and reabsorption, reintegration in the only reality, primeval Consciousness, Śiva, as pure unshakable potentiality.[43]

A Gandhāra object, recently published and interpreted by Tucci, may throw a new light on this secret ritual. It represents a three-faced stand in which three images are carved out. One of these images is shown in the act of masturbation. On the top of the stand there is an empty rectangular cavity in which, it seems probable, the *kuṇḍagolaka* was collected. According to Tucci's interpretation, this Gandhāra image conveys the metaphysical conceptions of the rituals of a Tantric school, the Akula.[44] "Gandhāra was a Śaivite centre and some peculiar Śaiva schools (like the Krama school) were developed in Swāt."[45] The importance of this ceremonial object is enhanced by its antiquity: first century or beginning of the second century A.D. This means that the secret sexual practices documented in later Tantric texts "were current already in some schools, to which we cannot so far give a name beyond contention, that existed in some parts of the North-Western region of the Indo-Pakistani Subcontinent, in the 1st, or the beginning of the 2nd cent. A.D."[46]

The Joyful Paradox

Ritual intercourse, the collection of genital emissions, and their ceremonial consumption as a sacrament have also been practiced by one of the licentious Gnostic sects, the Phibionites. We shall discuss their extravagant theology after analyzing the sequence God–spirit–light–seed in Iran and among the Gnostics (see below, pp. 109–12). But we should not conclude these notes on Tantric *maithuna* without emphasizing once more its ceremonial character. The insistence with which the Tantric authors emphasize that *maithuna* is quite another type of enterprise than profane sexual intercourse must be taken seriously. The only conclusion seems to be that those who practice it without previous spiritual and technical preparation will not discover in *maithuna* more than any ordinary sexual intercourse can offer. On the other hand, we must always keep in mind that the basic Tantric doctrine, in both the Hindu and Buddhist traditions, is paradoxical in character. Already in Upanishadic times, the saving *gnosis* was sufficient to "project" the *rishi* beyond the good and the evil. "One who knows this, although he commits very much evil, consumes it all and becomes clean and pure, ageless and immortal" (*Bṛhadāraṇyaka Up.* V. 14. 8). As the Tantric author Indrabhuti states: "By the same acts that cause some men to burn in hell for thousands of years, the yogin gains his eternal salvation."[47] The Buddhist Tantras are philosophically based on the *mādhyamika* doctrine of the unity of Nirvāṇa and *saṃsāra*, of the Absolute (or "ultimate reality") and human experience (or "nonbeing"). The realization of such a union of opposites always converges in a paradoxical situation. The Hindu *jīvan-mukta*, the "liberated in life," lives in time yet shares in immortality; he is in life and yet "liberated," etc.[48] No less paradoxical is the situation of a Boddhisattva, who, although he

> has his abode in Nirvāṇa, manifests himself in *saṃsāra*, he knows that there are no (human) beings, but he tries hard to convert them; he is definitively pacified (*śānta*); but he enjoys objects of desire (*kāmaguṇa*). He delights in the joys of *dharma*, but he openly gathers round himself woman, songs and plays, etc.[49]

For the Indian mind, absolute freedom (*samādhi, Nirvāṇa*, etc.) can be translated, admittedly in a rather imperfect way, only through a series of coincidences of opposites. No wonder that, among the methods proposed for conquering such a paradoxical mode of being, the most severe asceticism and innumerable techniques of meditation coexist with *maithuna* and the consumption of *kuṇḍagolaka*.

Xvarenah and the Seminal Fluid

According to the tradition preserved in *Dēnkart*, a Pahlavi book of the ninth century A.D., three nights before Zarathustra's birth his mother was so radiant that the entire village was illuminated. Thinking that a great fire had broken out, many inhabitants hurriedly left the village. Coming back later on, they found that a boy full of brilliance had been born.[50] Likewise, at the birth of Frīn, Zarathustra's mother, the house appeared to be on fire. Her parents saw her enveloped in a great light. When Frīn was fifteen years old, she radiated light whenever she moved. The text explains that her great radiance was due to the *xvarenah* (*xvar*) which was in her.[51]

The savior's mother receives from on high the incandescent light that will flow in Zarathustra's body and will sanctify it. But when such legends were written down, the biography of the prophet-savior was already almost completely mythologized. Thus it was stated that Zarathustra was born from *haoma*,[52] the divine liquid analogous to the Vedic *soma*. And, as we shall see, *haoma* was "full of *xvarenah*." In the last analysis, *xvarenah* is represented as a sacred, seminal, luminous, and fiery fluid.

Although articulated systematically only in late treatises, this conception is certainly much older. In the Gāthic and Avestic texts, the *xvarenah* eminently characterizes divine beings. In the *Yašt* dedicated to Mithra it is stated that from the forehead of the god "goes forth the flaming fire that is the strong royal *xvarenah*."[53] Another *Yašt* (XIX. 10) explains that Ahura Mazdah possesses *xvarenah* in order to "create all the creatures";[54] or, as *Dēnkart* puts it, to protect his Creation.[55] Although specifically and insistently related to sovereignty, the *xvarenah* is not restricted exclusively to kings.[56] Every human being has his own *xvarenah*; and at the final, eschatological renovation (*fraša*), this supernatural light will adorn all of them: "The great light appearing as coming forth from the body will shine continually over the earth. . . . And [this light] will be their garment, resplendent, immortal, exempt from old age."[57]

The texts do not seem to agree on the original source and the permanent abode of the *xvarenah*. But all the texts emphasize its supraterrestrial nature. Ohrmazd produces *xvarenah* from the infinite lights and preserves it in fire and water.[58] According to the Pahlavi book *Zātspram* (35. 82), "the abode of *xvarenah* is in the fire Varhrān," the royal fire par excellence.[59] But a much older text (*Yašt* VI. 1 ff.) states that "when the Sun burns, the gods distribute the *xvarenah*"; and this remark is important, for it clearly indicates the solar origin of the holy fluid. As a matter of fact, the etymology proposed already a century ago related the term *xvarenah* to *hvar*, "sun," and thus, to Sanskrit *svar*.[60] It only seems a paradox that other texts assert that *xvarenah* resides in the waters and especially in the Vouru.kaša Sea (see, for instance, *Yašt* VIII). It is said that the goddess Anāhitā has a great quantity of *xvarenah* and that her river brings this iridescent fluid from the top of the mountain Hukairya down into the Vouru.kaša Sea.[61] Moreover, the white *haoma* is represented in the Pahlavi texts as being found in the waters and is identified with Gōkarn, the tree of life, situated in the middle of Vouru.kaša. But the white *haoma* is "full of *xvarenah*," and it is also a recipient of *xvarenah*.[62] The seeming paradox of a fiery substance residing in water presents no difficulty if we keep in mind that the waters symbolize the infinite possibilities of life and fertility and also the source of "immortality."[63] We find a similar situation in Vedic cosmology: Agni is described as existing in the Waters; and Soma, though of celestial origin, is proclaimed the essence of life (the "seed" par excellence) and the provider of immortality. The human and animal seed is consequently both "fiery" and "liquid." The Pahlavi texts confirm the structural relation of *xvarenah* to "seed."[64] The *Great Bundahišn* I. 41 states that the animal and human seeds are made from fire, while all the rest of creation was produced from a drop of water.[65]

"Thus," concludes Gnoli, "the seed is not simply tantamount to light; the seminal fluid is not the luminous principle, the irradiant splendour; but it is the substance that contains this principle, and it is also its vehicle."[66] All the luminescent values of the seed derive from the "creative" nature of *xvarenah*. Indeed, *xvarenah* is not only "holy" (divine, supraterrestrial), "powerful" (it really "makes" the kings and heroes), "spiritual" (it engenders intelligence, bestows wisdom), and "solar" (and thus "fiery" and iridescent); but it is also "creative." Of course, the light is "cosmogonic" by its own mode of being. Nothing can "really *exist*" before the appearance of light. (Consequently, as we shall see [p. 107], the cosmic annihilation, wished for by the Gnostics and the Manichaeans, can be accomplished only through a long and complicated process of "extraction" of light particles, dispersed throughout the world, and their final reabsorption in a transcendent, acosmic "height.") But the creativity of the luminous principle is self-evident only for an alert intellect. Cosmogony and, in general, creation of different forms of life are mythically conceived as procreation, or divine "work." The seminal character of the luminous principle emphasizes the creativity, the fertility, and the inexhaustible ontophanies of the divine light.

Manichaeism: The Imprisoned Light

We do not need to recall the complex cosmogonic, anthropogonic, and eschatological myths of Manichaeism.[67] Although he utilized Iranian and Mesopotamian (Mandaean) elements, Mani produced his own basic mythology, as so many important Gnostics did before and after him, and as William Blake still ventured to do in the eighteenth century. Furthermore, Mani constructed a mythology according to the contemporary *Zeitgeist*, which demanded a long, intricate, pathetic divine and cosmic drama, having recourse to emanations, reduplications, macromicrocosmic homologies, and so on. The episode that interests us is the one at the very beginning of the cosmic drama, in which a portion of the divine light is captured by the power of darkness.

Realizing that the Prince of Darkness (= the Evil Principle) is ready to attack the realm of Light, the Father of Greatness decides to forgo confronting the adversary himself. He "evokes," that is, emanates, the Mother of Light, who, in her turn, projects a new hypostasis, the Primeval Man. Together with his five sons—who are, in fact, his own being, an armor consisting of five lights—the Primeval Man descends to the frontier; but he is conquered by Darkness, and his sons are devoured by the Demons. This defeat is the beginning of the cosmic "mixture," but it is also the guarantee of God's (Light's) final triumph. For now Darkness (Matter) possesses particles of Light, and the Father of Greatness, preparing their release, prepares at the same time the definitive victory over Darkness. In a second creation, the Father "evokes" the Living Spirit, who, proceeding to the boundary of Darkness, grasps the hand of the Primeval Man and raises him to the Paradise of Light, his celestial home. Vanquishing the demonic Archons, the Living Spirit makes the skies from their skins and the earth from their flesh and excrement. He also carries out a first liberation of Light, creating the Sun, the Moon, and the Stars from those parts which had not suffered too much as a consequence of their contact with Darkness.

Finally, in order to rescue the still-captive particles of Light, the Father emanates the Third Messenger. This messenger establishes a gigantic cosmic wheel that, in the first part of the month, draws up the rescued particles of Light toward the Moon, in a "column of glory." During the second half of the month, the Light is directed from the Moon to the Sun and finally to the Paradise of Light. But there are still those particles which have been swallowed by the Archons. Consequently, the Third Messenger shows himself to the male Archons in the shape of a radiant, beautiful, naked virgin, while to the female Archons he appears as a nude, shining youth. Overpowered by sexual desire, the male Archons discharge their sperm and, with their sperm, the particles of Light. From the seeds falling on the earth, trees and plants emerge. The female demons, already pregnant, miscarry at the sight of the beautiful youth. Thrown to earth, these abortions devour tree buds, thus assimilating particles of Light.[68]

Alarmed by the Third Messenger's tactics, Matter, personified in "Concupiscence," decides to create a stronger prison for the remaining divine particles. A male demon and a female demon, Aš-qualūn and Namrāel, devour all the monstrous abortions and then have intercourse. Thus were begotten Adam and Eve. As Puech puts it, "notre espèce naît donc d'une suite d'actes répugnants de cannibalisme et de sexualité" (*Le Manichéisme*, p. 80). But in Adam is now gathered the largest quantity of the remaining captive Light. Accordingly, Adam and his descendants become the central subject of redemption.

We will not recall the story of his salvation, which is modeled on the rescue of the primeval man. But, of course, the demonic nature of sexuality was the logical consequence of this myth of man's origin. Indeed, sexual intercourse and, especially, procreation are evil, for they prolong the captivity of light in the body of the descendant.[69] For a Manichaean, the perfect life means an uninterrupted series of purifications, that is to say, separations of spirit (light) from matter. The redemption corresponds to the definitive separation of light from matter, in the last analysis, to the end of the world.

"Mixture" and "Separation"

The Iranian and even the Indo-Iranian elements of the central Manichaean myth have been analyzed with increasing precision by
scholars of the past hundred years. The religious importance of
light-semen, the theory of the cosmic "mixture," the conception of
the "three times" (the time before the attack, the present time, and
the *eschaton*), the "seduction of the Archons," and many other
episodes have their antecedents or parallels in Iranian religions.[70]
The ideology of "separation," that is, the will to put an end to the
state of "mixture" (*gumešcin*), characterizes Iranian religions from
the earliest times to the rigid orthodoxy of the Sassanids. In a recent
article, Gnoli explains the function of the Zarathustrian sacrifice
(*yasna*) as ultimately promoting this soteriological "separation."[71]
By correctly practicing the *yasna*, the sacrificer is able to obtain the
condition of *maga*, a kind of "active trance," which confers upon
him a power (*xšathra*) of magical character and therefore a mystical
ability to see (*čisti*), a knowledge of supernormal realities, inaccessible to the bodily senses.[72] In this state the sacrificer "separates"
his spiritual essence (*mēnōk*) from his concrete, corporeal being
(*gētē*) and identifies himself with the Ameša-Spenta.[73] Moreover,
in the state of *maga*, that is, of "purity," man is "pure will"
(*axvapēčak*) and can exercise his "lordship" (*axvīh*), for he has
effectuated the transformation (*fraškart*), passing from the plane of
the existence *gētē*, under the dominion of fate (*baxt*), to that of the
existence *mēnōk*—of free action (*kunišn*). According to Gnoli, this
conception is at the basis of the Mazdaic doctrine of free will
(*āzātkām*), which proclaims that it is possible to deliver oneself
from the chains of Heimarmene and enter the reign of freedom.[74]

If Gnoli's interpretation of *yasna* is correct, it follows that a
"mystical" (that is, both "ecstatic" and "Gnostic") technique of
"separation" was known in Iran from the beginnings of Zoroastrianism. It is pointless to emphasize the difference between this
maga-theology and the Manichaean doctrine and practice of "separation." The capital distinction concerns the origin, meaning, and
purpose of the creation of cosmic life and of human existence. For
Zarathustra, the creation was not the work of demonic Archons but

of Ahura Mazdah. The world was corrupted afterward; for this reason, the ''separation'' is the first duty of every believer.

This is not the place to discuss the wide-ranging problem of the origin and history of so many religions, philosophies, sects, and gnoses centered on the idea of ''separation'' and promising the means to achieve it. It suffices to say that roughly from the sixth century B.C. in India and Iran and from the fifth century in the Greco-Oriental world, a number of metaphysics, soteriologies, and mystical techniques endeavoring to obtain absolute freedom, wisdom, or redemption implied ''separation'' as either a preliminary stage or the ultimate goal (e.g., Sāṃkhya-Yoga, Buddhism, Zoroastrianism, Orphism, and, in Hellenistic and early Christian times, Gnosticism, Hermetism, alchemy, etc.). It is especially in Gnosticism that the ideology and techniques of ''separation'' have been abundantly elaborated. And almost always the model of Gnostic redemption is formulated in terms of Light being separated from Darkness.[75] With minor, although sometimes significant, variations, all the Gnostic texts present a mythologized theology, a cosmogony, an anthropology, and an eschatology similar or parallel to the Manichaean ones. At least some of the most important Gnostic sects precede chronologically Mani's missionary activity. Gnosticism as well as Manichaeism considered the world to have been created by demonic powers, the Archons, or by their leader, the Demiurge. The same Archons later created man for no other reason than to keep captive the *pneuma*, the divine ''spark'' fallen from on high. In order to ''awaken'' man and release his *pneuma*, messengers are said to descend from the world of Light and to reveal the saving *gnosis*. Redemption means essentially the deliverance of this divine, celestial ''inner man'' and his return to his native realm of Light.[76]

The Phibionites: Sanctification through Semen

Through the possession of *gnosis*, the *pneumatikoi* consider themselves free from the human condition, beyond social rules and ethical interdictions—a situation which has parallels in other parts of the world, but especially in India. Indeed, the freedom of the

Gnostics to practice asceticism or sexual libertinage reminds one of
the Upanishadic *rishis* and the Tantric yogins. The most striking
parallel to the Śaiva and Tantric sexual rites discussed above (pp.
99–102) is certainly that of the Gnostic sect of the Phibionites.
Our main source is Epiphanius, who, as a young man, frequented
the meetings of the Phibionites in Alexandria and read several of
their books.[77] At their meetings, writes Epiphanius,

> they serve rich food, meat and wine even if they are poor.
> When they thus ate together and so to speak filled up their
> veins, from the surplus of their strength they turn to excitements.
> The man, leaving his wife, says to his own wife: "Stand up
> and make love with the brother" ("Perform the *agapē* with
> the brother"). Then the unfortunates unite with each other, and
> as I am truly ashamed to say the shameful things that are being
> done by them . . . , nevertheless I will not be ashamed to
> say those things which they are not ashamed to do, in order that
> I may cause in every way a horror in those who hear about their
> shameful practices. After they have intercourse in the passion
> of fornication they raise their own blasphemy toward heaven.
> The woman and the man take the fluid of the emission of the
> man into their hands, they stand, turn toward heaven, their
> hands besmeared with the uncleanness, and pray as the people
> called *Stratiotikoi* and *Gnostikoi*, bringing to the Father of the
> Nature of All, that which they have on their hands, and they
> say: "We offer to thee this gift, the body of Christ." And then
> they eat it, their own ignominy, and say: "This is the body of
> Christ and this is the Passover for the sake of which our bodies
> suffer and are forced to confess the suffering of Christ."
> Similarly also with the woman: when she happens to be in the
> flowing of the blood they gather the blood of menstruation of
> her uncleanness and eat it together and say: "This is the
> blood of Christ."[78]

Such strange and ignominious rites were related to the Phibionites' cosmology and theology. According to them, the Father (or
the Primordial Spirit) brought forth Barbelo (also called
Prounikos), who lived in the eighth heaven. Barbelo gave birth to
Ialdabaoth (or Sabaoth), the creator of the lower world. Con-

sequently, everything which was created and was alive, first and foremost the Archons—the rulers of the lower world—held a spark of Barbelo's power. But when she heard Ialdabaoth saying, "I am the Lord and there is no other, etc." (Isa. 45:5), Barbelo understood that the creation of the world had been an error and began to cry. In order to regain as much power as she could, "she appeared to the Archons in a beautiful form, seduced them, and when they had an emission she took their sperm, which contained the power originally belonging to her."[79] Thus, the salvation was hoped for and effectuated within a cosmic perspective. The Nicolaitans already proclaimed, "We gather the *dynamis* of Prounikos from the bodies through the fluids of the begetting power (*gonē*) and the menstrual blood" (*Panarion* 25. 3. 2). The Phibionites went even farther:

> the power which is in menstruation and in the sperm they called *psyche*, which would be gathered and eaten. And whatever we eat, flesh or vegetables or bread or anything else, we do a favor to the creatures because we gather the *psyche* from everything [. . . .] And they say that it is the same *psyche* which is dispersed in animals and beasts, fishes, snakes, men, vegetables, trees and anything that is produced. [*Panarion* 26. 9. 3–4.]

For this reason procreation is both an error and a crime; it divides the *psyche* again and prolongs its sojourn in the world.[80]

One can say that the ultimate goal of the Phibionites' sexual rituals was, on the one hand, to accelerate the reintegration of the precosmogonic stage, that is, the "end of the world," and, on the other hand, to approach God through a progressive "spermatization." Indeed, not only is the sperm sacramentally eaten, but, according to Epiphanius, when they become wild (ecstatic?) during their ceremonies, they smear their hands and bodies with their own emissions and "they pray that, through this practice, they may find with God free conversation."[81]

As Leisegang has pointed out, theological justification could be found in the First Epistle of John (3:9): "No one born of God commits sin; for the sperm of God abides in him, and he cannot sin

because he is born of God." Moreover, according to the Stoic
doctrine of *logos spermatikos*, understood as a fiery *pneuma*, the
human seed contains a *pneuma*, thanks to which the soul is formed
in the embryo.[82] The Stoic theory was the logical consequence of
Alcmaeon of Crotona's locating the seed in the brain,[83] that is, in
the same organ in which the soul, *psyche*, was supposed to reside.
As Onians points out, for Plato the *psyche* is "seed," *sperma*
(*Timaeus* 73c), "or rather is in the 'seed' (91a), and this 'seed' is
enclosed in the skull and spine (73 ff.). . . . It breathes through
the genital organ (91b). . . . That the seed was itself breath or
had breath (*pneuma*) and that procreation itself was such a breath-
ing or blowing is very explicit in Aristotle."[84]

Coming back to the Phibionites, we are still insufficiently informed about their rituals and beliefs to make an adequate comparison with the Tantric *maithuna* evoked by Abhinavagupta and the
Śaiva ceremonial of *kuṇḍagolaka*. All of these systems seem to
have in common the hope that the primordial spiritual unity can be
reconstituted through erotic bliss and the consumption of semen and
the menses. In all three systems the genital secretions represent the
two divine modes of being, the god and the goddess; consequently,
their ritual consumption augments and accelerates the sanctification
of the celebrants. But in all these schools, the original homologiza-
tion, divinity–spirit–light–sperm, is intermingled with other archaic
and no less relevant conceptions (e.g., the divine biunity, with its
implicit religious importance of the female element, the spiritual an-
drogynization of the celebrant, etc.).

A Morphology of Photisms

Thus, summing up, we find the following dominant ideas:

1. "Separation" of divine spirit (light) from matter (demonic
darkness) is a dominant theme in religious and philosophical speculations and in mystical techniques of Hellenistic and early Christian
times, but it is witnessed earlier in Iran and India.

2. Roughly in the same period, the equations God (spirit) =
light, and primordial man (spirit, *pneuma*) = light become ex-

tremely popular among the Gnostics, Mandaeans,[85] Hermetics,[86] and Manichaeans. Both equations seem to be characteristic of the Hellenistic *Zeitgeist*, and they contrast with the spiritual horizons of classical Greece, the Old Testament, and Christianity.

3. For the Gnostics[87] and the Manichaeans, redemption is tantamount to collecting, salvaging, and carrying to heaven the sparks of the divine light which are buried in living matter, first and foremost in man's body.

4. Although known by some other Gnostic sects,[88] the equation divine light = *pneuma* = semen plays a central role only among the Phibionites (and sects related to them) and among the Manichaeans. But while the latter, on the ground of this very equation, scorned the sexual act and exalted a severe asceticism, the Phibionites extolled the most abject sexual orgies and practiced the sacramental absorption of *semen virile* and menstrual fluids, careful only to avoid pregnancy. Similar divergent orientations—extreme asceticism on the one hand and orgiastic rituals on the other—are to be found in India from the times of the Upanishads; and, again only in India, among some Śaiva and Tantric sects, the ceremonial eating of genital secretions is witnessed (see above, pp. 99–102).

5. Ecstatic experiences of lights of different colors during *maithuna* are quoted by some Tantric authors (see pp. 99–100). Tucci infers Manichaean influences; but similar photic experiences, involving different colors in a specific order, are frequent during yogic meditations (see above, p. 96). They are also known in Taoist yoga and alchemy, and in Tibet they are said to be experienced during the agony of death and immediately afterward (see above, p. 100).

6. Photisms induced by sexual union and, in general, experiences of different "mystical" colors are not quoted in the available Gnostic documents; the only important allusion which I know of is the ecstatic journey described in the *Paraphrase of Shem* (no. 27 in the library discovered at Chenoboskion). Recalling the visions of his ecstatic ascent, Shem speaks of the clouds of different colors through which he has passed: "thus, the cloud of the Pneuma is like a sacred beryl; the cloud of Hymen is like a resplendent emerald;

the cloud of Silence is like a delightful amaranth; and the cloud of Mesotes is like a pure hyacinth."[89]

The ecstatic experience of lights of different colors will play an important role in Islamic, especially Ismaili, mysticism, whose relations with the Hellenistic gnosis and Iranian traditions have been convincingly pointed out by Henry Corbin.[90] Photic experiences were witnessed among the Sufis from early times.[91] However, it is especially with Najmoddîn Kobrâ (1220) that visions of colored lights began to be systematically described and interpreted as specific moments in an ecstatic itinerary. It suffices to read the passages from the great work of Najmoddîn Kobrâ, *Fawâ'ih al-jamâl wa-fawâtih al-jalâl* (= *Les Eclosions de la beauté et les parfums de la Majesté*), translated and brilliantly interpreted by Corbin,[92] to realize that we are confronted with a new and grandiose revalorization of the well-known experience of varicolored mystical lights. But, so far as I can judge from the documents presented and discussed by Corbin, the "seminal" value of Light seems to have been ignored, although the cosmogonic and cosmological themes are still present.[93]

A South American Example: "Sun-Father," Photic-Sexual Symbolism, and Hallucinatory Visions

A surprising parallel to some of the light-theologies discussed above is to be found among the Desanas, a small Tucano-speaking tribe living in the equatorial forests of the Vaupés River in Colombian Amazonia. The Desanas represent a rather archaic level of culture, disparaging fishing and horticulture and extolling hunting. Since I have discussed the ensemble of the Desanas' religious ideas and institutions elsewhere,[94] I shall limit the present notes to an analysis of the cultic role played by the eternally existing "Sun-Father" and the scope of his creativity.

From Sun-Father's golden and yellow light the entire creation emanated. The Creator-Sun is not really identical with the existing luminary in the sky but is, rather, the creative principle which continues to exist as such and which, although invisible, can be known through the beneficent influence which emanates from it.

Having concluded his creative activity, Sun retired to *Axpikon-día*, which is the subterranean paradisial zone. He did, however, send as his representative the luminary which we see today in the firmament and through which he continues to exert his power by bestowing light, warmth, protection, and, especially, fertility.[95] Sun's energy is expressed through the warm and golden light, which has the character of semen.[96] All of the divine figures were created by Sun-Father in order to protect his creation. These intermediaries are representatives of Sun. Ultimately, therefore, all the cosmic energies, the universal life, and all fertility are dependent upon the Sun-Father.[97]

According to a myth recently published by Reichel-Dolmatoff,[98] mankind was engendered by drops of semen fallen from the solar rays. Then Sun-Father enjoined a certain mythical personage, Pamuri-maxë, to guide the ancestors of the Vaupés River tribes to the territories they actually inhabit today. The voyage was made in a huge canoe, which was also a giant serpent. The sexual symbolism implied by this is confirmed by the etymology of the name Pamuri, a word which suggests an ejaculating phallus—that is, Sun-Father sending a new creator to populate the earth.[99]

Sex is the source of life, but it can also bring death, chaos, and destruction. Sun-Father committed incest with his daughter; she subsequently died, but he was able to resurrect her by fumigating her with tobacco smoke.[100] This crime of incest was followed by a period of chaos, a period during which beasts and demons appeared in great numbers and endangered the very life of the world. But the creator reestablished order by proclaiming the prohibition of incest; he thus made the first and most important socioethical rule.[101]

According to the Desanas, the soul is a luminous element which possesses its own luminosity, bestowed by Sun at the birth of every human being. When a soul is dangerously menaced by magical forces, three classes of solar lights are evoked in order to reinforce it. The second of these lights is white and is associated with the seminal powers of Sun. The internal luminosity of the soul is visible only to the initiates, that is, to shamans (*payé*) and priests (*kumú*).[102]

The soul of a *payé* is compared to a fire whose light penetrates the obscurity and makes everything visible; it is imagined as a flame that emits a mighty golden light, similar to that of Sun. A *payé* does not have power without the knowledge that is given by the light, for "he is a part of the Sun's light." Like the solar light, the light of the shaman's soul is gold-yellow; in other words, it "represents the fertilizing virtues of the Sun." [103] Every *payé* wears, suspended from his neck, a cylinder made from yellow or white quartz, called "Sun's phallus." Moreover, any quartz or crystal represents the *semen virile*. [104] The priest (*kumú*) is said to be, even more than the *payé*, a luminous personage. He emits a great amount of inner light, a brilliant flame—invisible to the noninitiates—with which he discovers everyone's thoughts. [105]

Thus, for the Desanas (and this is true for all the Tucano tribes of the Vaupés area), Sun-Father represents not only a creative high god but also the *fons et origo* of all the sacredness in the universe. Consequently, there is an intimate connection between solar light, holiness, creativity, and sex. All religious ideas, personages, and activities bear also a sexual signification. The reason for this hierophanic pansexualism may be looked for in the identification of solar light and solar warmth with the origin and perpetuation of cosmic and human life. The Sun-Father is one with the ground of being: his cosmic as well as his spiritual activity is a consequence of his ontological plenitude. He creates by emanation, and this type of cosmogony and theogony is also the exemplary model for man's own spiritual activity. Sun-Father remains invisible, although the solar light is the source of life and wisdom; likewise, the inner light of priest and shaman cannot be seen but can be perceived in and through its results.

Inasmuch as the sun's light is conceived as a divine, procreative *semen virile*, it is understandable that the ecstatic iridescent visions provoked by the hallucinogenic plant *yagé* have been compared with a sexual act. The Tucanos say that during coition man is "suffocated" and "sees visions." [106] According to a myth, the *yagé*-Woman was impregnated through the eyes. As a matter of fact, the equivalence eyes = vagina is familiar to the Tucanos. The verb "to fertilize" derives from the roots "to see" and "to deposit." [107]

The ceremonial drinking of *yagé* is carried out three or four times a year. The times themselves are decided on by the priest (*kumú*), who, at a feast or a reunion, announces that *yagé* will be taken. Only men of thirty years of age or more are allowed to participate. The women are present and encourage the celebrants by their songs;[108] they also laugh contemptuously whenever one of the younger men, overcome by nausea, hurriedly leaves the hut. The myth of the cult's origin tells that the supernatural *yagé*-Woman gave birth to a child who had "the form of light: he was human, yet he was Light; it was *yagé*."[109]

Before and during the drinking of *yagé*, the cosmogonic myth and mythical tribal genealogies are ceremonially recited. The role of the priest (*kumú*) is predominant, for he explains to the participants the visions they are experiencing. At the very beginning, the participant feels a strong wind blowing; he is told by the *kumú* that he is ascending to the Milky Way. He then descends to the *Axpikon-día*, the subterranean paradise, and sees increasingly more powerful golden lights, until he has the impression of a rain of luminous bodies. The second phase begins with the arrival in the subterranean paradise, when he perceives multiple forms of different colors; the *kumú* explains that these are various divine beings and Sun's daughter.

Taking *yagé* is expressed by a verb meaning "drink and see," and it is interpreted as a *regressus* to the cosmic womb, that is, to the primeval moment when Sun-Father began the creation. In fact, the visions recapitulate the theogony and cosmogony: the participants see how Sun-Father created the divine beings, the world, and man and how the tribal culture, the social institutions, and ethical norms were founded. The goal of the *yagé* ceremony is to strengthen religious belief; indeed, the participant can *see* that the tribal theogony and cosmogony are *true*. Besides, the visions permit a personal encounter with the supernatural beings, an encounter which is interpreted in sexual terms. A native who was educated by the missionaries explains: "Taking *yagé* is a spiritual coitus; is the spiritual communion, as the priests say."[110] On the other hand, it is also said that the one who takes *yagé* "dies,"[111] because the return to the cosmic womb is equivalent to death.

This is not the place to discuss the relations between the hallucinatory experiences and the Tucano theology and mythology.[112] The priest (*kumú*), who transmits the traditional meaning of the visions to the younger generations, plays a decisive role. But the foundation of the entire religious system is the theologoumenon of Sun-Father and, as a consequence, the connaturality of light, spirit, and semen. If everything which exists, lives, and procreates *is* an emanation of Sun, and if "spirituality" (intelligence, wisdom, clairvoyance, etc.) partakes of the nature of solar light, it follows that every religious act has, at the same time, a "seminal" and a "visionary" meaning. The sexual connotations of light-experiences and hallucinatory visions appear to be the logical consequence of a coherent solar theology. Indeed, in spite of its dominant sexual symbolism, the ceremonial drinking of *yagé* does not have any orgiastic aspect. The hallucinatory experience is valorized essentially for its ecstatic and luminous nature; its erotic significations derive from the solar theology, that is, from the fact that Sun-*Father engendered* everything and that, consequently, the solar light *is* "seminal."

The example of the Desanas admirably illustrates how a specific type of solar religion can valorize the light-experiences and integrate the hallucinatory visions in the structures of an ecstatic universe. Some of the Desanas' equivalences (e.g., light = sperm) remind one of Oriental and Mediterranean expressions. But this South American example also has the merit of calling our attention to the poverty of existing documents from the Oriental and Mediterranean areas. In fact, compared with the well-articulated theology, mythology, and hallucinogenic ritual of the Desanas, the Tantric and Gnostic texts seem, even the best of them, approximate and incomplete.[113]

Finally, the Desana example shows us in what sense and to what degree ecstatic experiences, hallucinatory or not, can enrich and restructure a traditional religious system. It appears that the series of equivalences light–spirit–semen–god, etc., remains "open"; that is to say, the original basic photic experiences are susceptible of receiving new meanings. Moreover, it appears that the inducing of photisms is not limited to a single agent; witness, as agents, the following: extreme asceticism, or the sexual act, or yogic and other contemplative practices; spontaneous photic explosions; heroic techniques pursuing the production of "magical heat"; systematic meditation on fire, solar light, and creativity; ecstatic and hallucinogenic visions, etc. In the last analysis, what is important is the religious meaning given to the experiences of inner light. In other words, the "origin" of *religiously meaningful* photisms is not to be sought for in the "natural causes" of the phosphenes or in the *experience* of such spontaneous or artificially induced phosphenes. This is so for the simple reason that, as recent studies have abundantly proved,[114] (1) phosphenes of different forms and colors are universally known and (2) these phosphenes can be induced through multifarious means, from simple physical pressure on the eyelids to the most refined techniques of meditation. What interests a historian of religion, and, as a matter of fact, a historian *tout court*, are the countless valorizations of light-experiences, that is to say, the *creativity* of the human mind.

Notes

Chapter 1

1. See, e.g., Léon Cellier, "Le Roman initiatique en France au temps du romantisme," *Cahiers Internationaux de Symbolisme*, no. 4 (1964), pp. 22–44; Jean Richer, *Nerval: Expérience et création* (Paris, 1963); Maryla Falk, *I "Misteri" di Novalis* (Naples, 1939); Erika Lorenz, *Der metaphorische Kosmos der modernen spanischen Lyrik, 1936–1956* (Hamburg, 1961).

2. I discussed some of these interpretations in my article "Initiation and the Modern World," reprinted in *The Quest: History and Meaning in Religion* (Chicago, 1969), pp. 112–26.

3. Sigmund Freud, *Totem und Tabu* (1913), p. 110, quoted by A. L. Kroeber, "Totem and Taboo: An Ethnological Psychoanalysis," *American Anthropologist* 22 (1920): 48–55.

4. Wilhelm Schmidt, *The Origin and Growth of Religion*, trans. H. J. Rose (New York, 1931), p. 112.

5. See Mircea Eliade, "The History of Religions in Retrospect: 1912–1962," reprinted in *The Quest*, pp. 12–36.

6. Schmidt, *Origin and Growth of Religion*, pp. 112–15.

7. Summarized by W. Robertson Smith, *Lectures on the Religion of the Semites*, rev. ed. (London, 1899), p. 338.

8. Ibid.

9. Ibid., p. 281.

10. See the bibliography in Joseph Henninger, "Ist der sogennante Nilus-Berich eine brauchbare religionsgeschichtliche Quelle?" *Anthropos* 50 (1955): 81–148, esp. pp. 86 ff.

11. G. Foucard, *Histoire des religions et méthode comparative*, 2d ed. (Paris, 1912), pp. 132 ff.

12. Ibid., p. lxv: "Et pour le chameau de saint Nil, je persisterai à croire qu'il n

mérite pas de porter sur son dos le poids des origines d'une partie de l'histoire des religions."

13. Karl Heussi, *Das Nilusproblem* (Leipzig, 1921). The bibliography of Heussi's work on Nilus is presented and discussed by Henninger, "Ist der sogenannte Nilus-Bericht . . . ," pp. 89 ff.

14. See the bibliography in Henninger, pp. 86 ff.

15. For a critical appraisal of the neopositivism of Lévi-Strauss see Georges Gusdorf, "Situation de Maurice Leenhardt ou l'ethnologie française de Lévy-Bruhl à Lèvi-Strauss," *Le Monde Non Chrétien* 71/72 (July/December 1964): 139–92. See also Paul Ricoeur, "Symbolique et temporalité," in *Ermeneutica e Tradizione*, ed. Enrico Castelli (Rome, 1963), pp. 5–31; Gaston Fessard, S.J., "Symbole, Surnaturel, Dialogue," in *Demitizzazione e Morale*, ed. Enrico Castelli (Padua, 1965), pp. 105–54.

16. Mircea Eliade, "The Sacred and the Modern Artist," *Criterion*, spring 1965, pp. 22–24. The article was originally published as "Sur la permanence du sacré dans l'art contemporain," *XXe Siècle*, no. 24 (December 1964), pp. 3–10.

Chapter 2

1. B. Spencer and F. J. Gillen, *The Arunta*, 2 vols. (London, 1926), 1:388.

2. Cf. Mircea Eliade, *The Sacred and the Profane* (New York, 1959), pp. 31–39. See also id., *Australian Religions: An Introduction* (Ithaca, N.Y., 1973), pp. 50–53.

3. Claude Lévi-Strauss, *Tristes tropiques* (Paris, 1955), pp. 227 ff.; Joseph Rykwert, *The Idea of a Town*, reprinted from *Forum*, Lectura Architectonica (Hilversum, n.d.), p. 41.

4. *Aeneid* 4. 212; cf. Rykwert, *The Idea of a Town*.

5. Cf. *The Sacred and the Profane*, p. 47; see also Eliade, "Centre de Monde, Temple, Maison," in R. Bloch et al., *Le Symbolisme cosmique des monuments religieux* (Rome, 1957), pp. 57–82; Paul Wheatley, *The City as Symbol* (London, 1967); id., *The Pivot of the Four Quarters: A Preliminary Inquiry into the Origins and Character of the Ancient Chinese City* (Chicago, 1971).

6. See Stella Kramrish, *The Hindu Temple*, 2 vols. (Calcutta, 1946), 1:14 ff., 26 ff., and passim; see also our forthcoming book, "The Center of the World."

7. See the sources to be quoted in "The Center of the World."

8. Bernard-Philippe Groslier and Jacques Arthaud, *The Arts and Civilization of Angkor* (New York, 1957), p. 30.

9. For the references, see "The Center of the World," chap. 2.

10. See Mircea Eliade, *The Quest: History and Meaning in Religion* (Chicago, 1969), pp. 77 ff., 160 ff.

11. See our article " 'Briser le toit de la maison': Symbolisme architectonique et physiologie subtile," in *Studies in Mysticism and Religion, Presented to Gershom*

G. Scholem, ed. E. E. Urbach, R. J. Zwi Werblowsky, and C. Wirszubski (Jerusalem, 1967), pp. 131–39, and "The Center of the World," chaps. 3–4.

12. See *The Sacred and the Profane*, pp. 46, 73–74.

13. See J.-P. Lebeuf, *L'Habitation des Fali montagnards du Cameroun septentrional* (Paris, 1961), pp. 457 ff.

14. See the sources quoted in Eliade, *The Myth of the Eternal Return* (New York, 1959), pp. 7 ff., and in *The Sacred and the Profane*, pp. 36 ff.

15. Jonathan Z. Smith, "Earth and Gods," *Journal of Religion* 49 (1969): 112.

16. Quoted, ibid., p. 113.

17. Ibid., p. 117.

18. Ibid., p. 118.

19. Quoted, ibid., p. 120, n. 41.

20. Quoted, ibid., p. 119.

21. Ibid., pp. 125–26.

22. But see also Richard L. Rubenstein, "The Cave, the Rock, and the Tent: The Meaning of Place," *Continuum* 6 (1968): 143–55.

Chapter 3

1. W. Lloyd Warner, *A Black Civilization: A Study of an Australian Tribe* (1937; rev. ed., 1958; reprint, New York, 1964), pp. 5–6.

2. On myths of the origin of death, see J. G. Frazer, *Folklore in the Old Testament*, 3 vols. (London, 1919), 1:45–77; Theodor H. Gaster, *Myth, Legend and Custom in the Old Testament* (New York, 1969), pp. 35–47, 339–40; Mircea Eliade, *From Primitives to Zen: A Thematic Sourcebook of the History of Religions* (New York, 1967), pp. 139–44.

3. Australian tribes: cf., *inter alia*, T. G. H. Strehlow, *Aranda Traditions* (Melbourne, 1947), pp. 44–45 (myth reproduced in *From Primitives to Zen*, pp. 140–42).

Central Asiatic, Siberian, and North American mythologies: see some examples in Mircea Eliade, *Zalmoxis, the Vanishing God*, trans. Willard R. Trask (Chicago, 1972), pp. 76 ff.

4. See Hans Abrahamsson, *The Origin of Death: Studies in African Mythology* (Uppsala, 1951).

5. R. H. Codrington, *The Melanesians* (Oxford, 1895), p. 265 (= *From Primitives to Zen*, p. 139).

6. J. G. Frazer, *The Belief in Immortality*, 3 vols. (London, 1913), 1:74–75, quoting A. C. Kruijt (= *From Primitives to Zen*, p. 140).

7. Cf. M. Eliade, *Myths, Dreams, and Mysteries*, trans. Philip Mairet (New York, 1960; reprinted, New York, 1967), pp. 59 ff. See also id., *Australian Religions: An Introduction* (Ithaca, N.Y., 1973), pp. 33 ff.

8. See, *inter alia*, Olof Pettersson, *Jabmek and Jabmeaimo: A Comparative Study of the Dead and of the Realm of the Dead in Lappish Religion* (Lund, 1957), pp. 20 ff.

9. G. Reichel-Dolmatoff, "Notas sobre el simbolismo religioso de los Indios de la Sierra Nevada de Santa Maria," *Razón y Fabula, Revista de la Universidad de los Andes*, no. 1 (1967), pp. 55–72, esp. pp. 63 ff. See also M. Eliade, *The Quest: History and Meaning in Religion* (Chicago, 1969), pp. 138 ff.; id., "South American High Gods, Part II," *History of Religions* 10, no. 3 (1971): 234–66, esp. pp. 256 ff.

10. Cf. M. Eliade, *Birth and Rebirth*, trans. Willard R. Trask (New York, 1958); reprinted as *Rites and Symbols of Initiation* (New York, 1965).

11. *Birth and Rebirth*, pp. 15 ff.

12. M. Eliade, *Shamanism: Archaic Techniques of Ecstasy*, trans. Willard R. Trask (New York, 1964), pp. 500 ff.

13. See ibid., pp. 213 ff., 311 ff., 368 ff. See also R. A. Stein, *Recherches sur l'epopée et le barde au Tibet* (Paris, 1959), pp. 317 ff., 370 ff.

14. There is a considerable literature on these themes. The works of Frazer (*The Belief in Immortality*, vols. 1–3) and Olof Pettersson (*Jabmek and Jameaimo*) are valuable for the materials collected (see the bibliography in Pettersson, pp. 233–41). For a rather summary presentation see F. Bar, *Les Routes de l'autre monde* (Paris, 1946).

15. M. Eliade, *Australian Religions*, p. 167.

16. Buecheler, ed., *Carmina latina epigraphica*, no. 1421, quoted by J. P. Jacobsen, *Les Manes*, 3 vols. (Paris, 1924), 1:72.

17. Oscar Cullmann, "Immortality of the Soul or Resurrection of the Dead?" in Krister Stendahl, ed., *Immortality and Resurrection* (New York, 1965), p. 29.

18. For examples see M. Eliade, *Méphistophélès et l'Androgyne* (1962), pp. 171 ff. (= *Mephistopheles and the Androgyne* [New York, 1965], pp. 137 ff.).

19. I discuss these mythical geographies in a book in preparation, "Mythologies de la mort."

20. See Jan de Vries, *Untersuchung über das Hüpfspiel: Kinderspiel-Kulttanz*, Folklore Fellows Communication no. 173 (Helsinki, 1957), pp. 83 ff. See also Siegbert Hummel and Paul G. Brewster, *Games of the Tibetans*, Folklore Fellows Communication no. 187 (Helsinki, 1963), pp. 18–19, 32–33.

21. *Mūlamadhyamakakānikās* 25. 19, translated by Frederick J. Streng, *Emptiness* (Nashville, 1967), p. 217.

22. Martin Heidegger, *Sein und Zeit*, p. 250, with the commentary of William J. Richardson, *Heidegger: Through Phenomenology to Thought* (The Hague, 1967), p. 76.

23. Richardson, *Heidegger*, p. 574.

24. Heidegger, *Vorträge und Aufsätze* (Pfullingen, 1954), p. 177, with the commentary of Richardson, *Heidegger*, pp. 573–74.

Chapter 4

1. There is a considerable literature on the occult and the occult revival. One can consult Richard Cavendish, *The Black Arts* (New York, 1967); Colin Wilson, *The Occult* (New York, 1971); Edward F. Heenan, ed., *Mystery, Magic, and Miracle: Religion in a Post-Aquarian Age* (Englewood Cliffs, N.J., 1973); Richard Woolly, *The Occult Revolution: A Christian Meditation* (New York, 1973); Martin Marty, "The Occult Establishment," *Social Research* 37 (1970): 212–30; Andrew M. Greeley, "Implications for the Sociology of Religion of Occult Behavior in the Youth Culture," *Youth and Society* 2 (1970): 131–40; Marcello Truzzi, "The Occult Revival as Popular Culture: Some Random Observations on the Old and Nouveau Witch," *Sociological Quarterly* 13 (winter, 1972): 16–36 (with a rich bibliography); Edward A. Tiryakian, "Toward the Sociology of Esoteric Culture," *American Journal of Sociology* 78 (November 1972): 491–512; id., "Esotérisme et exotérisme en sociologie: La sociologie à l'âge du Verseau," *Cahiers Internationaux de Sociologie* 52 (1952): 33–51. See also Edward A. Tiryakian, ed., *On the Margin of the Visible: Sociology, the Esoteric, and the Occult* (New York, 1974); Robert Galbreath, "The History of Modern Occultism: A Bibliographical Survey," *Journal of Popular Culture* 5 (winter, 1971): 726–54, reprinted in *The Occult: Studies and Evaluation* (Bowling Green, Ohio, 1972).

2. Tiryakian, "Toward the Sociology of Esoteric Culture," pp. 498 f.

3. Ibid., p. 499.

4. On Eliphas Lévi, see Richard Cavendish, *The Black Arts*, pp. 31 ff.

5. On Papus, see René Guénon, *Le Théosophisme, histoire d'une pseudo-religion* (Paris, 1921), pp. 202 ff.

6. See Gérard van Rijnberk, *Un Thaumaturge au XVIIIe siècle: Martines de Pasqually, sa vie, son oeuvre, son ordre*, 2 vols. (Paris, 1935, 1938).

7. On Louis-Claude de Saint-Martin, "Le Philosophe Inconnu," see Antoine Faivre, *L'Esotérisme au XVIIIe siècle* (Paris, 1973), pp. 188 ff., and the bibliography quoted on p. 201, n. 125.

8. *Revue Illustrée*, 15 February 1890, quoted by Lucien Méroz, *René Guénon ou la sagesse initiatique* (Paris, 1962), p. 28.

9. Cf. Richard Cavendish, *The Black Arts*, pp. 34 ff.

10. Ibid., pp. 37 ff.; cf. J. Symonds, *The Great Beast* (New York, 1952). See also *The Confessions of Aleister Crowley: An Autobiography*, ed. John Symonds and Kenneth Grant (New York, 1969).

11. Cf. Tiryakian, "Toward the Sociology of Esoteric Culture," pp. 504 ff.

12. On René Daumal, see Jean Biès, *Littérature française et pensée hindoue, des origines à 1950* (Paris, 1974), pp. 491 ff, and bibliography pp. 670 f.

13. See especially H. Corbin, *En Islam iranien*, 4 vols. (Paris, 1971–72).

14. Cf. René Le Forestier, *La Franc-Maçonnerie Templière et occultiste* (Paris, 1970); Alice Joly, *Un Mystique lyonnais et les secrets de la Franc-Maçonnerie* (Mâcon, 1938); Gérard van Rijnbeck, *Un Thaumaturge au XVIIe siècle*; Antoine

Faivre, *Kirchberger et l'illuminisme du 18ᵉ siècle* (The Hague, 1966); id., *Eckartshausen et la théosophie chrétienne* (Paris, 1969); id., *L'Esotérisme au XVIIIᵉ siècle* (Paris, 1973).

15. See Nathan Sivin, *Chinese Alchemy: Preliminary Studies* (Cambridge, Mass., 1968); cf. M. Eliade, "Alchemy and Science in China," *History of Religions* 10 (November 1970): 178–82. After these lines were written, Joseph Needham brought out the fifth volume of his magnificent work, *Science and Civilization in China* (Cambridge, Eng., 1974), dedicated to "Spagyrical Discovery and Invention: Magisteries of Gold and Immortality."

16. M. Eliade, *The Forge and the Crucible: The Origins and Structures of Alchemy* (New York, 1971); the book was originally published under the title *Forgerons et alchimistes* (Paris, 1956).

17. Cf. M. Eliade, *Yoga: Immortality and Freedom* (New York, 1958); originally published in French (Paris, 1954); Agehananda Bharati, *The Tantric Tradition* (London and New York, 1963); Alex Wayman, *The Buddhist Tantras* (New York, 1973).

18. See M. Eliade, *Shamanism: Archaic Techniques of Ecstasy* (New York, 1964); originally published in French (Paris, 1951); cf. the bibliography, pp. 518–69.

19. To illustrate the broad interest in shamanism, I will cite only two recent publications: *Hallucinogens and Shamanism*, ed. Michael J. Harner (New York, 1973), and the sumptuous issue of *Artscanada*, nos. 184–87 (December 1973/January 1974), entitled *Stones, Bones, and Skin: Ritual and Shamanic Art*, with profuse illustrations.

20. Frances A. Yates, *Giordano Bruno and the Hermetic Tradition* (Chicago, 1964); id., "The Hermetic Tradition in Renaissance Science," in Charles S. Singleton, ed., *Art, Science and History in the Renaissance* (Baltimore, 1967), pp. 255–74; id., *The Theater of the World* (Chicago, 1967); id., *The Rosicrucian Enlightenment* (London, 1972). See also Peter J. French, *John Dee: The World of an Elizabethan Magus* (London, 1972).

21. See below, chap. 5, "Some Observations on European Witchcraft."

22. Carlo Ginsburg, *I Benandanti* (Turin, 1966).

23. Cf. below, "Some Observations on European Witchcraft."

24. Edward F. Heenan, ed., *Mystery, Magic and Miracle*, p. 87. See also Milbourne Christopher, *ESP, Seers and Psychics* (New York, 1970), pp. 101 ff.; Marcello Truzzi, "The Occult Revival as Popular Culture," pp. 19 ff.; Edward A. Tiryakian, "Toward the Sociology of Esoteric Culture," pp. 494 ff.; Martin Marty, "The Occult Establishment," pp. 217 ff.

25. Tatian *Oratio ad Grecos* 4. 9; cf. M. Eliade, *The Myth of the Eternal Return* (New York, 1954), pp. 132 ff.

26. See M. Christopher, *ESP, Seers, and Psychics*, pp. 109 ff.

27. Philippe Defrance, Claude Fischler, Edgar Morin, and Lena Petrosian, *Le Retour des astrologues* (Paris, 1971).

28. Tiryakian, "Toward the Sociology of Esoteric Culture," p. 496.

29. Brought out in 1969, *The Satanic Bible* was followed by *The Compleat Witch* (New York, 1971). See also LaVey's declarations, recorded by John Fritscher, "Straight from the Witch's Mouth" (in Edward F. Heenan, ed., *Mystery, Magic and Miracle*, pp. 89–107). Professor E. J. Moody, after being a member of the First Church of Satan in San Francisco for two and a half years while doing participant observation, published a notable paper, "Magical Therapy: An Anthropological Investigation of Contemporary Satanism," in *Religious Movements in Contemporary America*, edited by Irving I. Zaresky and Mark P. Leone (Princeton, 1974), pp. 355–82. According to Moody, "the would-be Satanist expresses his problem in terms of lack of power" (p. 364):

In addition to teaching the novice Satanist magic, his fellow witches and magicians teach him that he is "evil," but the definition of evil is changed. . . . He is actively encouraged to speak of his evil (deviant) thoughts and deeds and lauded instead of reviled for them. It is a tenet of the Satanic theology that evil is relative to the time and place in which the deed is done. . . . It is the position of the Satanic Church that the "white light magicians" (Christians) made sins of natural human impulses in order to be sure that people would transgress. They then, by making salvation dependent on belief in Christianity, "hooked" the populations and made them dependent on the Christian Church for freedom from fear. The Satanists, by contrast, persuade their new members to revel in their own humanity, to give free reign to their natural impulses and indulge their appetites without fear or guilt. Members are constantly reminded that man is the human *animal*, and members are encouraged to throw off the shackles of Christianity and rediscover the joy of living. (P. 365.)

Of course, this joy of living is organically related to a noninhibited sexuality. One recognizes the pattern of old European antinomian movements, as well as traits of more modern orientations (for instance, those of A. Crowley, J. Evola, etc.).

30. "The University of California, on June 16, 1970, gave the first Bachelor of Arts degree in Magic ever conferred in this country" (Heenan, in Edward F. Heenan, ed., *Mystery, Magic, and Miracle*, p. 88). See also Truzzi, "The Occult Revival," pp. 23 ff.; Marty, "The Occult Establishment," pp. 215 ff.; Edward F. Heenan, "Which Witch? Some Personal and Sociological Impressions," in *Mystery, Magic and Miracle*, pp. 105–18; Arthur Lyons, "The Twisted Roots," in *Mystery, Magic, and Miracle*, pp. 119–38.

31. Robert S. Ellwood, Jr., *Religious and Spiritual Groups in Modern America* (Englewood Cliffs, N.J., 1973), pp. 179 ff. See also Egon Larsen, *Strange Sects and Cults: A Study of Their Origins and Influence* (New York, 1971); Peter Rowley, *New Gods in America* (New York, 1971); William J. Peterson, *Those Curious New Cults* (New Canaan, 1973); William Braden, *The Age of Aquarius: Technology and the Cultural Revolution* (Chicago, 1970).

32. Ellwood, *Religious and Spiritual Groups*, p. 179.

33. Ibid., p. 104.

34. Ibid., p. 203. A more complex, and highly successful, "new religion,"

bringing together a therapeutic technique, based on a rather ambitious theory of the mind, with some elements from traditional occultism, is Scientology, founded by L. Ron Hubbard. See George Malko, *Scientology: The Now Religion* (New York, 1970); Harriet Whitehead, "Scientology, Science Fiction, and Occultism," in Irving I. Zaresky and Mark P. Leone, eds., *Religious Movements in Contemporary America*, pp. 547–87.

35. Ellwood, *Religious and Spiritual Groups*, p. 195.

36. Robert S. Ellwood, "Notes on a Neopagan Religious Group in America," *History of Religions* 11 (August 1971): 138. In his booklet *The Kore* (Feraferia, Inc., 1969), Frederick Adams relates the reemergence of the feminine archetype, the heavenly nymphet, with the Age of Aquarius:

To inform the dawning Eco-Psychic Age of Aquarius, wherein celebration will determine subsistence, a long repressed image of divinity is re-emerging: the Merry Maiden, Madonna, Rima, Alice in Wonderland, Princess Ozma, Julia, Lolita, Candy, Zazie of the Metro, Brigitte, Barbarella, and Windy—a grotesque and incongruous assemblage at first sight—are all early harbingers of the Heavenly Nymphet. She alone may negotiate free inter-action between the other three anthropomorphic divinities of the Holy Family. These are the Great Mother, who dominated the Old and New Stone Ages; the Great Father, who initiated the Early Patriarchal Era; and the Son, who crystalized the megalopolitan mentality of the Late Patriarchal Era. It is the Dainty Daughter of the Silver Crescent who will transmute the saturate works of Father and Son to wholeness in the Material Ground of Existence, without sacrificing the valid achievements of masculine articulation. And She accomplishes this without a crippling imposition of parental or heroic authority images. How delightful to behold her tease and tickle Father and Son into respectably natural, Life-affirming pagan Gods again. (Quoted by Ellwood, "Notes," p. 134.)

37. As a matter of fact, as Theodore Roszak and Harvey Cox have pointed out, the entire youth (counter) culture is oriented to a radical, "existential" *renovatio*. The phenomenon is not without precedents in relatively recent European history. Some of the specific traits of contemporary youth movements characterize also the famous pre–World War I German youth movement, the Wandervögel. See Nathan Adler, "Ritual, Release, and Orientation," in Irving I. Zaresky and Mark P. Leone, eds., *Religious Movements in Contemporary America*, pp. 288–89.

38. See M. Eliade, *Birth and Rebirth: Meanings of Initiation in Human Culture* (New York, 1958); reprinted as *Rites and Symbols of Initiation* (New York, 1965), pp. 115 ff.

39. See Lucien Méroz, *René Guénon ou la sagesse initiatique*.

40. We hasten to add that this doctrine is considerably more rigorous and more cogent than that of the occultists and hermeticists of the nineteenth and twentieth centuries. For an introduction to it, see Méroz, *René Guénon*, pp. 59 ff. See also Jean Biès, *Littérature française et pensée hindoue*, pp. 328 ff., and the bibliography on pp. 661 f.

41. R. Guénon, *La Métaphysique orientale* (Paris, 1937), pp. 12 ff.

42. See, *inter alia*, the essays by Frithjof Schuon, Marco Pallis, Titus Burckhardt, and others, in *The Sword of Gnosis: Metaphysics, Cosmology, Tradition, Symbolism*, ed. Jacob Needleman (Baltimore, 1974).

Chapter 5

1. Etienne Delcambre, *Le Concept de la sorcellerie dans le duché de Lorraine au XVIᵉ et XVIIᵉ siècle* (Nancy, 1948–51); H. R. Trevor-Roper, *The European Witch-Craze of the Sixteenth and Seventeenth Centuries and Other Essays* (New York, 1969), a Harper Torchbook which reprints chaps. 1–4 of *The Crisis of the Seventeenth Century: Religion, the Reformation and Social Change* (1968); Jeffrey Burton Russell, *Witchcraft in the Middle Ages* (Ithaca, N.Y., 1972), with a rich bibliography (pp. 350–77); Keith Thomas, *Religion and the Decline of Magic* (New York, 1971). See also E. W. Monter, ed., *European Witchcraft* (New York, 1969); id., "The Historiography of European Witchcraft: Progress and Prospects," *Journal of Interdisciplinary History* 2 (1972): 435–51.

2. Joseph Hansen, *Zauberwahn, Inquisition und Hexenprozess im Mittelalter und die Enstehung der grossen Hexenverfolgung* (Munich, 1900; reprint ed., Munich, 1964); and *Quellen und Untersuchungen zur Geschichte des Hexenwahns und der Hexenverfolgung im Mittelalter* (Bonn, 1901; reprint ed., Hildesheim, 1963); H. C. Lea, *The History of the Inquisition in the Middle Ages*, 3 vols. (New York, 1883; reprint ed., New York, 1957); and *Materials toward a History of Witchcraft*, ed. Arthur Howland, 3 vols. (Philadelphia, 1939; reprint ed., New York, 1957).

3. Hansen, *Zauberwahn*, p. 328; cf. Russell, *Witchcraft in the Middle Ages*, p. 34.

4. Cf. *History of the Inquisition*, 3:539; Russell, p. 31. On George Lincoln Burr, see Russell, pp. 32 and 298, n. 9.

5. See Montague Summers, *The History of Witchcraft and Demonology* (London, 1926; reprint ed., New York, 1956); *The Geography of Witchcraft* (London, 1927); *Witchcraft and Black Magic* (London, 1946). Summers' books are "erratic and unreliable, but not without value" (Russell, *Witchcraft in the Middle Ages*, p. 30).

6. See, e.g., M. Eliade, *Yoga: Immortality and Freedom* (New York, 1958), pp. 296 ff., 419 ff.

7. Failings aggravated in her later works: *The God of the Witches* (London, 1934; 2d ed., 1952); *The Divine King in England* (London, 1954).

8. Elliot Rose, *A Razor for a Goat: A Discussion of Certain Problems in the History of Witchcraft and Diabolism* (Toronto, 1962), p. 16. In a footnote (*The European Witch-Craze*, p. 116, n. 1), Trevor-Roper writes: "The fancies of the late Margaret Murray need not detain us. They were justly, if irritably, dismissed by a real scholar as 'vapid balderdash' (C. L. Ewen, *Some Witchcraft Criticism*, 1938)."

9. Russell, *Witchcraft in the Middle Ages*, p. 37.

10. The idea of a "pact" to renounce Christ and to honor the Devil appeared for the first time in the eighth century (see ibid., pp. 65 ff.).

11. Carlo Ginzburg, *I benandanti: Ricerche sulla stregoneria e sui culti agrari tra cinquecento e seicento* (Turin, 1966).

12. Ibid., pp. 8–9.

13. Although they sometimes infringed it by loquacity or boasting (ibid., p. 19).

14. Ibid., p. 19 and n. 2. A rich bibliography on the beliefs and rituals related to the caul can be found in Thomas R. Forbes, "The Social History of the Caul," *Yale Journal of Biology and Medicine* 25 (1953): 495–508.

15. Ginzburg, *I benandanti* p. 18. While in prison, one of the accused was ready to retract; an angel told him that what they were doing was diabolic (p. 14).

16. See the documents quoted ibid., p. 28.

17. On this mythico-ritual scenario, cf. M. Eliade, *The Quest: History and Meaning in Religion* (Chicago, 1969), pp. 165 ff.

18. Ginzburg, *I benandanti* p. 34.

19. Ibid., p. 35.

20. Only in 1532 did some of these followers of Diana admit, under torture, to having profaned the Cross and the sacraments (see the documents cited by Ginzburg, ibid., p. 36).

21. See ibid., pp. 87 ff.

22. Ibid., p. 110.

23. Ibid., pp. 115 ff.

24. Ibid., pp. 133–34.

25. Ibid., pp. 148 ff. But even as late as 1661 some *benandanti* still had the courage to proclaim that they fought for the Christian faith against the *stregoni* (p. 155). In two cases of *maleficium* tried in 1384–90 in Milan, Russell recognizes some traces of beliefs analogous to those of the *benandanti* (Russell, *Witchcraft in the Middle Ages*, p. 212).

26. "Der Werwolf in Livland und das letzte im Bendeschen Landgericht und Dörptschen Hofgericht i. Jahr 1692 deshalb stattgehabte Strafverfahren," *Mitteilungen aus der livländischen Geschichte* 22 (Riga, 1924–28): 163–220.

27. (Frankfurt am Main, 1934), 1:345–51.

28. Wittenberg, 1580, pp. 133^v–134^r.

29. *I benandanti*, p. 40.

30. Cf., *inter alia*, Otto Höfler, *Verwandlungskulte, Volkssagen und Mythen* (Vienna, 1973), pp. 15, 234, and passim.

31. On *strigoi*, see the rich documentation brought together by Ion Muşlea and Ovidiu Bîrlea, *Tipologia folclorului: Din răspunsurile la chestionarele lui B. P. Hasdeu* (Bucharest, 1970), pp. 244–70. Less frequent is the belief that the *strigoi* anoint themselves with a special ointment and leave the house by the chimney (pp. 248, 256).

32. Ibid., p. 251.

33. The dead *strigoi* likewise assemble around midnight and fight among themselves with the same weapons as the living ones (ibid., pp. 267 ff.). As in many other European folk beliefs, garlic is considered the best defense against living or dead *strigoi* (ibid., pp. 254 ff., 268 ff.). In the *Corrector* of Burchard of Worms (eleventh century), it is forbidden to believe what some women claimed, namely, that "they go out at night through closed doors and fly up into the clouds *to do battle*" (Russell, *Witchcraft in the Middle Ages*, p. 82; italics added). But, as in the case of the Romanian *strigoi*, the *Corrector* does not state with whom the tenth-century women fought.

34. On the *Wilde Heer*, see Viktor Waschnitius, *Perht, Holda und verwandte Gestalten: Ein Beitrag zur deutschen Religionsgeschichte* (Vienna, 1914), esp. pp. 173 ff.; Otto Höfler, *Kultische Geheimbünde der Germanen*, 1:68 ff.; id., *Verwandlungskulte, Volkssagen und Mythen*, pp. 78 ff.; Waldeman Liungmann, *Traditionswanderungen: Euphrat-Rhein*, Folklore Fellows Communication no. 118 (Helsinki, 1937), pp. 596 ff.; R. Bernheimer, *Wild Men in the Middle Ages* (Cambridge, Mass., 1952), pp. 79 ff., 132; Ginzburg, *I benandanti*, pp. 48 ff.

35. On the etymology of *zîna* (< *Diāna*) and *zînatec* (< Lat. *dianātĭcus*), see the critical bibliography in Alejandro Cioranescu, *Diccionario etimológico Rumano* (Universidad de La Laguna, 1961), p. 915; Al. Rosetti, *Istoria limbii române* (Bucharest, 1968), pp. 367, 395. The name of a specific group of *zîne*, the Sînziene, derives probably from Latin **sanctae Diānae*. The *Sînziene*, who are rather friendly fairies, gave their name to the important feast of Saint John the Baptist (June 24).

36. See M. Eliade, *Zalmoxis: The Vanishing God* (Chicago, 1972), pp. 68 ff.

37. On *zîne* and *iele*, see, *inter alia*, I.-Aurel Candrea, *Folclorul românesc comparat* (Bucharest, 1944), pp. 156 ff.; Muşlea and Bîrlea, *Tipologia folclorului*, pp. 206 ff.

38. Cf. M. Eliade, "Notes on the Căluşari," in *The Gaster Festschrift, Journal of the Ancient Near Eastern Society of Columbia University* 5 (1973): 115–22.

39. On the medieval traditions related to Diana ("riding with Diana," etc.) and Herodiada, see Lea, *Materials toward a History of Witchcraft*, 1:177 ff., 190 ff., etc.; Russell, *Witchcraft in the Middle Ages*, pp. 47 ff., 75 ff., 157 ff., 210 ff., 235 ff. (theories about Diana). In the northwestern regions of the Iberian Peninsula, Diana appears occasionally in the company of certain spirits referred to as *dianae*; see Julio Caro Baroja, *The World of the Witches* (Chicago, 1964), p. 65; cf. the Romanian *Doamna Zînelor* and the *zîne*; see also the bibliography given in n. 34, above.

40. The most important documentary sources for the organization and rituals of the *căluşari* are Tudor Pampfile, *Sărbătorile de vară la Români* (Bucharest, 1910, pp. 54–75; Theodor T. Burada, *Istoria teatrului în Moldova*, 2 vols. (Jassy, 1905), 1:62–70. New materials are presented by Mihai Pop, "Consideraţii etnografice şi medicale asupra căluşului oltenesc," in *Despre medicina populară românească* (Bucharest, 1970), pp. 213–22; Gheorghe Vrabie, *Folclorul* (Bucharest, 1970), pp. 511–31; Horia Barbu Oprişan, *Căluşarii* (Bucharest, 1969). On the initiation and the oath-taking ceremony, see the sources quoted in Eliade, "Notes on the Căluşari," p. 116, nn. 5–6.

41. See Muşlea and Bîrlea, *Tipologia*, pp. 211 ff., Eliade, "Notes," pp. 117 ff.

42. Eliade, "Notes," p. 119.

43. Ibid.

44. E. N. Voronca, *Sărbătoarea Moşilor la Bucureşti* (1915), p. 92; Eliade, "Notes," p. 120.

45. See R. Vuia, "Originea jocului de căluşari," *Dacoromania* 11 (1922): 215–54; Eliade, "Notes," pp. 120 ff.

46. On the *Sântoaderi*, see S. F. Marian, *Sărbătorile la Români*, 2 vols. (Bucharest, 1889), 2:40 ff.; Octavian Buhociu, *Le Folklore roumain de printemps*, typewritten thesis University of Paris, 1957, pp. 164 ff.; Eliade, "Notes," pp. 120 ff.

47. Buhociu, *Le Folklore roumain*, pp. 180 ff.; Eliade, "Notes," pp. 121–22.

48. On the transformation of the dichotomies and polarities in a religious dualism implying the *idea of evil*, see Eliade, *The Quest*, pp. 173 ff.

49. Russell, *Witchcraft in the Middle Ages*, pp. 157–58.

50. J. B. Russell, *Dissent and Reform in the Early Middle Ages* (Berkeley and Los Angeles, 1965), pp. 27–35; id., *Witchcraft in the Middle Ages*, pp. 86 ff. See also Walter Wakefield and Austin P. Evans, *Heresies of the High Middle Ages* (New York, 1969), pp. 74 ff.

51. Russell, *Witchcraft in the Middle Ages*, p. 126.

52. See the documentation ibid., pp. 128–30, 318–19.

53. The sources are quoted and discussed ibid., pp. 141, 178 ff., 224.

54. Ibid., p. 161.

55. Ibid., p. 223.

56. Ibid., p. 224.

57. Ibid., pp. 250, 341, n. 61. Saint Peter was accused of having sacrificed a one-year-old infant, *puer anniculus*, to assure Christianity a duration of 365 years. The fact that Saint Augustine felt it necessary to answer such a calumny shows that, in the fourth century of our era, the pagan world still believed in the efficacy of such magical techniques. See J. Hubaux, "L'Enfant d'un an," in *Collection Latomus*, vol. 2: *Hommages à Joseph Bidez et à Franz Cumont* (Brussels, 1949), pp. 143–58; cf. J. Dölger, "Sacramentum infanticidii," in *Antike und Christentum* (Munster, 1929–50), 4:188–228.

58. Cf. Justin *Dialogue with Trypho* 10. 1.

59. See the references in Russell, *Witchcraft in the Middle Ages*, pp. 90–93; 314, nn. 48–50.

60. See the references cited in Eliade, *Yoga*, pp. 420–21.

61. Cf. Karl Konrad Grass, *Die russischen Sekten*, 3 vols. (Leipzig, 1905–14), 3:201 ff.

62. See M. Eliade, *Patterns in Comparative Religions* (New York, 1958), s.v. "ritual orgy." See also A. W. Howitt, *The Native Tribes of South-East Australia* (London, 1904), pp. 170, 195, 276 ff. (exchange of wives in order to avert an epidemic or at the appearance of the aurora australis); B. Spencer and F. J. Gillen, *The Northern Tribes of Central Australia* (London, 1904), pp. 136 ff.; id., *The Native Tribes of Central Australia* (London, 1899), 96 ff. (cf. also n. 65, below); Edward

Westermarck, *The History of Human Marriage*, 3 vols. (New York, 1922), 1:170 (on the annual feast of the Duśik Kurds in the Dersim Mountains: the orgy begins after the lights are extinguished), 231, 233 (the "wife-exchanging or lamp-extinguishing game" of the Eskimos), 235 (Philippines: orgies after marriages; Madagascar, after the birth of a child in the royal family); W. W. Rockhill, *The Land of the Lamas* (New York, 1891), pp. 80 ff. (the "hat-choosing festival" of the Amdo Tibetans); A. E. Crawley, *The Mystic Rose*, revised and greatly enlarged by Theodore Besterman, 3 vols. (New York, 1927), 1:362 ff. (Hawaii: at the funeral feasts, etc.).

63. Hans Schärer, *Ngaju Religion* (The Hague, 1963), pp. 94–95; cf. pp. 150, 159.

64. Cf. Eliade, *The Quest*, p. 85.

65. Cf. Eliade, *Australian Religions: An Introduction* (Ithaca, N. Y., 1973), pp. 46 ff.

66. Russell, *Witchcraft in the Middle Ages*, pp. 224 ff., 327, n. 21.

67. Cf. Steven Runciman, *The Medieval Manichee: A Study of the Christian Dualist Heresy* (Cambridge, Eng., 1946; reprint ed., New York, 1961), p. 96.

68. Ibid., p. 97.

69. M. Eliade, *Mitul Reintegrării* (Bucharest, 1942), pp. 24 ff.

70. See Baroja, *The World of the Witches*, p. 186. However, the ritual nudity and the ceremonial intercourse belong to the initiatory pattern of European witchcraft, and this tradition survived in the United States; see, e.g., Vance Randolph, *Ozark Superstitions* (New York, 1947), chap. 12, and "Nakedness in Ozark Folk Belief," *Journal of American Folklore* (1953).

Chapter 6

1. "Significations de la 'Lumière Intérieure,'" *Eranos-Jahrbuch* 25 (1957): 189–242, reprinted with additions in *Méphistophélès et l' Androgyne* (Paris, 1962), pp. 17–94, hereafter cited as *M & A*. Cf. also the English translation, *Mephistopheles and the Androgyne* (New York, 1965; reprinted in 1969 as a Harper Torchbook, with the title *The Two and the One*), pp. 19–77.

2. *M & A*, pp. 93–94; English translation, pp. 76–77 (slightly modified).

3. I shall not discuss here the larger systems into which these series of equivalences were integrated; for instance, the archaic and certainly Indo-Iranian pairs of opposites male and female and creative light ("breath," "intelligence") and dark, chaotic primeval waters, or the Vedic and Brahmanic cosmological speculations related to Agni and Soma. The series of equivalences we shall presently investigate are the results of specific spiritual experiences and theoretical systematizations which were eventually organized into a new morphology.

4. See also *Rig Veda* X. 82. 5–6; *Atharva Veda* X. 7. 28. Later on, the cosmogonic myth speaks of a golden egg.

5. *Jaiminīya Upaniṣad Brāhmaṇa* III. 10. 4–5.

6. *Taittirīya Saṁhitā* VII. 1. 1. 1; *Satapatha Brāhmaṇa* VIII. 7. 1. 16.

7. A. Coomaraswamy rightly equates *tiṣṭhan* with *instans*; cf. "'Spiritual Paternity' and the 'Puppet-Complex,'" *Psychiatry* 8 (August 1954): 25–35, esp. p. 26.

8. *Bṛhadāraṇyaka Up.* III. 7. 23; cf. III. 9. 28.

9. Cf. also *Kauṣītakī Brāhmaṇa Up.* I. 6: "I am produced as the seed for a wife, as the light of the year, as the self (*ātman*) of every single being." For other Indian texts, from the Upanishads to Rāmānuja, describing Brahman as pure light, see J. Gonda, *The Vision of the Vedic Poets* (The Hague, 1963), pp. 270 ff.

10. On impregnation by the sun, see E. S. Hartland, *Primitive Paternity*, 2 vols. (London, 1910), 1:25 ff., 89 ff. The significance of this mythological motif is corroborated by its integration and revalorization in Christian iconography. In a great number of Byzantine and Greek Orthodox icons, as well as in some famous Western nativities, a ray of light extends directly from the sun to the Virgin.

11. The most important documents are conveniently quoted and reproduced by Erwin Goodenough in *Jewish Symbols in the Greco-Roman Period*, 13 vols. (New York, 1956), 5:16 ff. and figs. 154 ff.

12. *Dīghanikāya* XIX. 15, trans. T. W. Rhys Davids, *Dialogues of the Buddha*, 2:264.

13. *Akārāṅga Sūtra* II. 15. 7 (= *Jaina Sūtras*, pt. 1, trans. Hermann Jacobi, in *Sacred Books of the East*, 50 vols. [Oxford, 1884], 22:191). The explanation given in the sequel to the Sūtra, that the light originated from "descending and ascending gods and goddesses," is a scholastic rationalization of an archaic and pan-Indian theme. The *Kalpa Sūtra*, 97, of Bhadrabāhu (ibid., p. 251) simply reproduces the text of *Akārāṅga Sūtra*.

14. *Lalitavistara*, I, p. 3, quoted and discussed by A. Coomaraswamy, "Līlā," *Journal of the American Oriental Society* (1941), pp. 98–101, esp. p. 100. See also E. Senart, *Essai sur la légende du Bouddha*, 2d ed. (Paris, 1882), pp. 126 ff., 149, etc. It does not matter if, in such texts, *uṣṇīṣa* already means (as Coomaraswamy had assumed) "cranial protuberance" or still means "turban"; Y. Krishan, in "The Hair on the Buddha's Head and Uṣṇīṣa," *East and West* 16, nos. 3–4 (September–December 1966): 275–89, came to the conclusion that "the literal meaning of the word *uṣṇīṣa* is a head wearing a cap or turban or a turban head." But, as Coomaraswamy rightly observes, "in either case it is from the top of the head that the light proceeds."

15. Cf. Senart, *Bouddha*, pp. 127 ff.; Gonda, *Vision of the Vedic Poets*, pp. 268 ff. See also Etienne Lamotte, *Le Traité de la Grande Vertu de sagesse de Nāgārjuna*, 2 vols. (Louvain, 1944), 1:431 ff., 527 ff., and passim.

16. H. Kern, *Histoire du bouddhisme dans l'Inde*, 2 vols. (Paris 1901–3), 1:69.

17. Ibid., 2:295.

18. Gonda, *Vision of the Vedic Poets*, pp. 274 ff.

19. See Etienne Lamotte, *L'Enseignement de Vimalakīrti* [*Vimalakīrti-nirdeśa*, trans. and annotated] (Louvain, 1962), p. 53. See also D. S. Ruegg, *La Théorie du Tathāgatagarbha et du Gotra: Etudes sur la sotériologie et la gnoséologie du*

bouddhisme (Paris, 1969), pp. 409–57 ("La Luminosité naturelle de la pensée"); G. Tucci and W. Heissing, *Les Religions du Tibet et de la Mongolie* (Paris, 1973), pp. 110 ff., 125 ff.

20. *Laṅkāvatāra*, pp. 77–78; Lamotte, *L'Enseignement*, p. 55.

21. In the theory of "thought nonthought" (*cittam acittam*) of the Prajñāpāramitā, the original nature of thought is still declared to be luminous; cf. Lamotte, *L'Enseignement*, p. 58. See also E. Conze, "Buddhism and Gnosis," in *The Origins of Gnosticism*, ed. Ugo Bianchi (Leiden, 1967), pp. 651–67, esp. p. 654, quoting G. Tucci, *Tibetan Painted Scrolls*, 3 vols. (Rome, 1949), 1:211: "For the Mahāyāna the intimate essence of man's being is 'the celestial nature itself, purest light, *boddhicittaṃ prakṛtiprabhāsvaram.*'" For the experience and meaning of the "Radiant Light" in Tibetan Buddhism, see Herbert V. Guenther, *The Life and Teaching of Naropa* (Oxford, 1963), pp. 69–72 (text); pp. 188–97 (translator's commentary).

22. I will not cite again the Chinese materials which I have already discussed in *M & A*, pp. 52–58 (English translation, pp. 45–49). Particularly interesting is the Taoist process of "absorbing the five-colored breaths," which are visualized as if they came from the four points of the compass and the center, that is to say, from the entire universe. This conception is archaic (cf., *inter alia*, M. Granet, *La Pensée chinoise* [Paris, 1934], pp. 151 ff., 342 ff., etc.; H. Köster, *Symbolik des chinesischen Universismus* [Stuttgart, 1958], pp. 50 ff.), and one must keep this in mind when investigating the problem of Iranian, that is, Manichaean, influences on neo-Taoism (cf. below, p. 113). No less important are the neo-Taoist techniques described in *The Secret of the Golden Flower*, especially the circulation of inner light inside the body and the production of the "true seed," which is eventually transformed into an embryo (*M & A*, pp. 56–57; English translation, pp. 46–48). Cf. also C. Hentze, "Lichtsymbolik und die Bedeutung von Auge und Sehen im ältesten China," *Studium Generale* 13 (1960): 333–51.

23. R. A. Stein, "Architecture et pensée religieuse en Extrême-Orient," *Arts asiatiques* 4 (1957): 180.

24. R. A. Stein, *La Civilisation tibétaine* (Paris, 1962), pp. 205–6.

25. For this reason the lama pulls out a few of the hairs directly over the sagittal suture; cf. W. Y. Evans-Wentz, *The Tibetan Book of the Dead*, 3d ed. (London, 1960), p. 18. On *brāhmarandhra*, see M. Eliade, *Yoga: Immortality and Freedom*, trans. Willard R. Trask (New York, 1958), pp. 234, 237, 243 ff.

26. R. A. Stein, "Architecture et pensée religieuse," p. 184; id., *La Civilisation tibétaine*, pp. 189 ff. Cf. M. Eliade, "'Briser le toit de la maison': Symbolisme architectonique et physiologie subtile," in *Studies in Mysticism and Religion, Presented to Gershom G. Scholem*, ed. E. E. Urbach, R. J. Zwi Werblowsky, and C. Wirszubski (Jerusalem, 1967), pp. 131–39.

27. *M & A*, pp. 48–49; English translation, pp. 41–43. According to a Tibetan monk, in the beginning men multiplied in the following way: the light which emanated from the body of the male penetrated, lit, and impregnated the womb of the

female. The sexual instinct was satisfied by sight alone. But men degenerated and began to touch one another with their hands, and finally they discovered sexual union. Cf. M. Hermanns, *Mythen und Mysterien, Magie und Religion der Tibeter* (Cologne, 1956), p. 16. See *M & A*, p. 48, n. 50; English translation, p. 42, n. 2, for other bibliographical references. Cf. G. Tucci, *Tibetan Painted Scrolls*, 2:711, 730–31. According to some Judeo-Christian and Gnostic traditions, after his "sin" (i.e., sexual union) Adam lost his original light; cf. B. Murmelstein, "Adam: Ein Beitrag zur Messiaslehre," *Wiener Zeitschrift für die Kunde des Morgenlandes* 35 (1928): 242–75, esp. p. 255, n. 3 (bibliographical information); E. Preuschen, "Die apocryphen gnostischen Adamschriften: Aus dem armenischen übersetzt und untersucht," in *Festgruss Bernhard Stade* (Giessen, 1900), pp. 165–252, esp. pp. 176, 187, 190, 205.

28. On the problem of Iranian influences on Tibet, see R. A. Stein, *Recherches sur l'épopée et le barde au Tibet* (Paris, 1959), pp. 390–91; F. Sierksma, "Rtsodpa: The Monacal Disputations in Tibet," *Indo-Iranian Journal* 8 (1964): 130–52, esp. 146 ff.; Matthias Hermanns, *Das National-Epos der Tibeter, gLing König Ge sar* (Regensburg, 1965), pp. 63 ff., 71 ff. In his monumental work *Tibetan Painted Scrolls*, G. Tucci discussed the Zurvanite, Manichaean, and Gnostic influences on Central Asiastic Buddhism, Tibetan Bon-pa, and Indo-Tibetan Tantrism; cf. Tucci, 1:711, 730 ff. See also below, p. 100.

29. See M. Eliade, *Yoga*, pp. 259 ff. However, there are exceptions; cf. Agehananda Bharati, *The Tantric Tradition* (London, 1965), pp. 265 ff.; Ferdinand D. Lessing and Alex Wayman, *Mkhas grub rje's Fundamentals of the Buddhist Tantras* (The Hague, 1968), p. 319.

30. Tucci, "Some Glosses upon the Guhyasamāja," *Mélanges chinois et bouddhiques* 3 (1935): 339–53.

31. See above, p. 97, and notes 14–21.

32. Tucci, "Some Glosses," p. 344; *M & A*, pp. 45–47; English translation, pp. 40–41.

33. Tucci, "Some Glosses," pp. 349–50; id., *Tibetan Painted Scrolls*, 1: 210 ff. Tucci considers that "even the identification of light with the mystic knowledge reminds us of the luminous *gnōsis* of the Manichaeans" ("Some Glosses," p. 350). But we have seen that such identification is much older and might go back to an Indo-Iranian tradition (see also below, p. 104 f.). On the other hand, Tucci points out the similarity between the Mahāyānic and the Gnostic division of people into three classes; cf. *Jñānamuktāvalī, Commemorative Volume in Honour of J. Nobel* (New Delhi, 1959), p. 226. E. Conze agrees with Tucci that his tripartite division denotes a Gnostic influence (see his "Buddhism and Gnosis," p. 655).

34. See M. Eliade, *Yoga*, pp. 254 ff.

35. Conze, "Buddhism and Gnosis," p. 657, reminds us that a few centuries before the Tantras, Sophia had been described, in some Hebrew speculations, as "suitable for sexual intercourse" (quoting H. Ringgren, *Word and Wisdom* [Uppsala, 1947], p. 119); later on, "the Gnostic Simon called his consort Helene, a harlot

he had found in a brothel in Tyre, by the names of 'Sophia' (= *prajñā*) or 'Ennoia' (= *vidyā*)."

36. See *M & A*, pp. 42–45; English translation, pp. 37–40.

37. See the examples quoted in *M & A*, pp. 17–18, 79–90; English translation, pp. 19–20, 66–75, mainly from R. M. Bucke, *The Cosmic Consciousness* (Philadelphia, 1901); R. C. Johnson, *The Imprisoned Splendour* (New York, 1953); Warner Allen, *The Timeless Moment* (London, 1946); and a series of articles by J. H. M. Whiteman, now reprinted in his book *The Mystical Life* (London, 1961). Some relevant psychedelic-mystical experiences have recently been brought into the discussion by R. E. L. Masters and Jean Houston (*The Varieties of Psychedelic Experience* [New York, 1967]), who state that only 6 of their 206 subjects had "mystical experiences" under the influence of the psychedelic drug. "In almost every case the experience is initiated with a sense of the ego dissolving into boundless being. This process is almost always attended by an experience of the subject being caught up in a torrent of preternatural light" (*Varieties*, p. 307). A forty-nine-year-old woman writes: "All around and passing through me was the Light, a trillion atomized crystals shimmering in blinding incandescence. I was carried by this Light to an Ecstasy beyond ecstasy" (ibid., pp. 307–8). A fifty-two-year-old engineer writes of an energy, neither hot nor cold, "experienced as a white and radiant fire" (ibid., p. 309). Another subject (a "highly sensitive and intelligent woman in her late fifties," who had studied Oriental religious literature for twenty-five years, had practiced meditation, knew of Huxley's experience with mescaline, and had hoped for something similar in taking LSD) states, "I became a diffused light that broke into a brilliant glittering, quivering thing—then it burst—bringing a shower of dazzling rays—each ray filled with a myriad of colors—gold, purple, emerald, ruby—and each ray charged with a current—throwing off sparkling lights—there was the ecstasy—all identification with self dissolved. There was no sense of time-space. Only an awareness of Being" (ibid., pp. 310–11).

38. Cf. Bharati, *The Tantric Tradition*, pp. 266 ff.

39. J. L. Masson and M. V. Patwardhan, *Śāntarasa and Abhinavagupta's Philosophy of Aesthetics* (Bhandarkar Oriental Research Institute, Poona, 1969), p. 43, quoting *Tantrāloka*, verse 137, p. 97. During the *maithuna*, writes Abhinava, "I do not exist, nor does anyone else" (verse 64, p. 44). According to Jayaratha's commentary, the goal of the sexual ritual is to "reveal" or "suggest" *ātmānanda* (Masson and Patwardhan, pp. 40–41).

40. On such "secret languages," see M. Eliade, *Yoga*, pp. 249 ff.; Bharati, *The Tantric Tradition*, pp. 164 ff.; D. L. Snellgrove, *The Hevajra Tantra*, 2 vols. (London, 1959), 1: 22 ff.

41. Masson and Patwardhan, *Śāntarasa*, p. 42, n. 1. But Abhinava and Jayaratha "are careful to point out that the reason for engaging in such rituals must be transcendental, and not be lust or greed" (ibid., n. 2).

42. *Tantrāloka* XXIX, stanzas 127–28, p. 92, quoted by G. Tucci, "Oriental Notes: III. A Peculiar Image from Gandhāra," *East and West* 18, nos. 3–4 (September–December 1968): 289–92, esp. p. 292, nn. 15–16.

43. Ibid., p. 292.

44. *Kula* means the *Śakti*, *akula* is *Śiva*; the *akulavīra* is a solitary hero; he is everything, "he is no Śiva and no Śakti, i.e., beyond them, one" (ibid., p. 290).

45. Ibid., p. 292 and n. 18.

46. Ibid., p. 292.

47. *Jñānasiddhi*, 15, quoted in Eliade, *Yoga*, p. 263.

48. Cf. *Yoga*, pp. 93 ff.

49. From the Chinese translation of *Avatamsaka* by Śikṣānanda, quoted by Lamotte, *L'Enseignement de Vimalakīrti*, p. 36 (my translation of Lamotte's text).

50. *Dēnkart* 7. 2. 56 ff.; cf. Marijan Molé, *Culte, mythe et cosmologie dans l'Iran ancien* (Paris, 1963), p. 289.

51. *Zātspram* 5, translated by Molé, p. 284; cf. *Dēnkart* 7. 2. 1 f. See also Henry Corbin, *En Islam iranien*, 4 vols. (Paris, 1972), 4:319 (at the birth of the twelfth Imām, his mother "resplendissait d'une lumière qui éblouissait les yeux").

52. See the texts quoted and discussed by Molé, *Culte, mythe, et cosmologie*, pp. 285 ff.

53. *Yašt* X. 127; I. Gershevitch dates the hymn in the second part of the fifth century B.C.; see his *The Avestan Hymn to Mithra* (Cambridge, Eng., 1959), p. 3; cf. G. Gnoli, "Un particulare aspetto del simbolismo della luce nel Mazdeismo e nel Manicheismo," *Annali dell' Istituto Orientale di Napoli*, n.s. 12 (1962): 95–128, esp. p. 99; J. Duchesne-Guillemin, "Le *Xvarenah*," *Annali dell' Istituto Orientale di Napoli, Sezione Linguistica* 5 (1963): 19–31, esp. pp. 22 ff.

54. Cf. Gnoli, "Aspetto," p. 106. On *xvarenah*, see also Gnoli, "Lichtsymbolik in Alt-Iran," *Antaios* 8 (1967): 528–49; R. C. Zaehner, *The Dawn and Twilight of Zoroastrianism* (London, 1961), pp. 150 ff.

55. See the texts quoted by Molé, *Culte, mythe, et cosmologie*, pp. 437 ff.

56. See ibid., p. 467. The possibility of Mesopotamian influences on the Iranian conception of sovereignty has been recently discussed by a number of scholars; see, *inter alia*, G. Widengren, "The Sacral Kingship of Iran," in *La Regalità Sacra* (Leiden, 1959), pp. 245–57; id., *Die Religionen Irans* (Stuttgart, 1965), pp. 151 ff., 310 ff., 342 ff.; R. N. Frye, "The Charisma of Kingship in Ancient Iran," *Iranica Antiqua*, 4 (1964): 36–54; J. Gonda, "Some Riddles Connected with Royal Titles in Ancient Iran," *Cyrus Commemoration Volume* 1 (1969): 29–46, esp. p. 45; G. Gnoli, "Politica religiosa e concezione della regalità sotto i Sassanidi," *La Persia nel Medioevo* (Rome, 1971), pp. 1–27, esp. pp. 20 ff. Morphologically, *xvarenah* can be compared with the Mesopotamian *melannu*, the "divine splendor" which is also characteristic of kings; cf. Elena Cassin, *La Splendeur divine* (Paris and The Hague, 1968), esp. pp. 65 ff. ("le *melannu* et la fonction royale"). For similar ideas in Egypt, Syria, and Greece see George E. Mendenhall, *The Tenth Generation: The Origins of Biblical Tradition* (Baltimore and London, 1973), pp. 32 ff. The probable source of such ideas seems to be the archaic and universally diffused conception of the supernatural radiance of divine and semidivine beings (see, *inter alia*, documents as different as *Hymn to Apollo* 440 ff., *Hymn to Demeter* 275 ff., and *Bhagavad Gītā* XI. 12 ff., etc.). It is likewise probable that the

traditional concept of "fortune" derives from beliefs similar to that of *xvarenah*; see Alessio Bombaci, "Qutlut Bolzun!" *Ural-Altäische Jahrbücher* 36 (1965): 284–91; 37 (1966): 13–43, esp. 36:22 ff.

57. *Zātspram*, translated by Molé, *Culte, mythe, et cosmologie*, p. 98; see also p. 475.

58. *Dēnkart*, 347, edited and translated by R. C. Zaehner, *Zurvān* (Oxford, 1955), pp. 359–71; cf. Molé, *Culte, mythe, et cosmologie*, p. 436; see other references in Gnoli, "Aspetto," p. 103.

59. See Duchesne-Guillemin, "Le *Xvarenah*," p. 26.

60. In 1943, however, H. W. Bailey in his learned book, *Zoroastrian Problems in the Ninth Century Books* (Oxford, 1943), proposed another etymology: "the good things of life." But Bailey's interpretation has been convincingly criticized by Duchesne-Guillemin ("Le *Xvarenah*," pp. 20 ff.) and by Gnoli ("Aspetto," p. 98).

61. See the texts quoted by Gnoli, "Aspetto," pp. 100–102.

62. For the most important references see ibid., p. 102.

63. See M. Eliade, *Traité d'histoire des religions* (Paris, 1949), pp. 173 ff.; Gnoli, "Lichtsymbolik," pp. 539 ff.; id., "Aspetto," p. 102.

64. Cf. *Dēnkart*, p. 347 (in Zaehner, *Zurvān*, pp. 369–71); Gnoli, "Aspetto," p. 103.

65. Zaehner, *Zurvān*, pp. 282–83; Gnoli, "Aspetto," pp. 110–11: "Ritorna dunque ancora una volta la concezione germinale delle luce e del fuoco come strumento e forma dentro cui la creazione a poco a poco si articola, sostanza, infine, dello spermo umano ed animale, che, unica cosa di tutto il creato, non procede della goccia di acqua primordiale" (p. 111).

66. Gnoli, "Aspetto," p. 121.

67. All the important facts and an exhaustive bibliography up to 1949 are to be found in H.-Ch. Puech, *Le Manichéisme* (Paris, 1949); see also Geo Widengren, *Mani and Manichaeism* (London, 1965; original German edition, 1961); for a history of the Western scholarly interpretation of Manichaeism from the beginnings of the nineteenth century, see R. Manselli, *L'eresia del male* (Napoli, 1963), pp. 10–27.

68. See F. Cumont, *Recherches sur le Manichéisme: I. La Cosmogonie manichéenne d'après Théodore bar Khôni* (Brussels, 1908), esp. "La Séduction des Archontes," pp. 54–68; W. Bousset, *Hauptprobleme der Gnosis* (Göttingen, 1907), pp. 76 f.; Puech, *Le Manichéisme*, pp. 79 f. and 173 f. (notes 324 f.).

69. See Puech, *Le Manichéisme*, p. 88.

70. See, *inter alia*, Widengren, *Mani and Manichaeism*, pp. 44 f., 54 f., 60 f.; id., *Die Religionen Irans* (Stuttgart, 1965), pp. 299 f.

71. "Lo stato di 'maga,'" *Annali dell' Istituto Orientale di Napoli*, n.s. 15 (1965): 105–17.

72. This Gāthic *čisti*, analogous to the Vedic *citti*, is the "spiritual vision" (*mēnōk-vēnišnih*) or "animic vision" (*jān-vēnišn*) discussed by the Pahlavi texts; cf.

Gnoli, "Lo stato di 'maga,'" p. 106; id., "La gnosi iranica: Per una impostazione nuova del problema," in Ugo Bianchi, ed., *The Origins of Gnosticism*, pp. 281–90, esp. p. 287.

73. This explains the double aspect, divine and, at the same time, human, of the Ameša-Spenta in the *gāthas* and the Pahlavi texts. This also explains the notion of *maga* as a state of "purity" or of "separation" (*apečakīh*), opposed to the state of "mixture" (*gumēčakīh, gumēcišn*); cf. Gnoli, "La gnosi iranica," p. 287.

74. Cf. "Lo stato di 'maga,'" pp. 114 f.; "La gnosi iranica," pp. 287 f.

75. Of course, in Hellenistic times Light was the typical verbal and iconographic equivalent of God or divine beings, and similar imageries were utilized in Judaism and early Christianity; see the bibliographies quoted in *M & A*, pp. 65 ff., and notes 86–95; English translation, pp. 55 ff. See also F.-N. Klein, *Die Lichtterminologie bei Philon von Alexandrien und in der hermetischen Schriften: Untersuchungen zur Struktur der religiösen Sprache der hellenistischen Mystik* (1962); C. Colpe, "Lichtsymbolik in alten Iran und antiken Judentums," *Studium Generale* 18, no. 2 (1965): 118 ff.

76. To quote Jonas, "On the scale of the total divine drama, this process is part of the restoration of the deity's own wholeness, which in precosmic times has become impaired by the loss of portions of the divine substance. It is through these alone that the deity became involved in the destiny of the world, and it is to retrieve them that its messenger intervenes in cosmic history" (Hans Jonas, *The Gnostic Religion*, 2d ed., enlarged [Boston, 1963], p. 45).

77. In *Panarion* 26. 8. 1, Epiphanius quotes the titles of some of these books: *Questions of Mary, Revelations of Adam, Book of Noria, Gospel of Eve*, etc.; cf. Stephen Benko, "The Libertine Gnostic Sect of the Phibionites according to Epiphanius," *Vigiliae Christianae* 2 (1967): 103–19, esp. pp. 104 ff. Jean Doresse, *Les Livres secrets des Gnostiques d'Egypte*, 2 vols. (Paris, 1958), 1:182 (= *The Secret Books of the Egyptian Gnostics* [New York, 1960], pp. 159, 163), states that *The Hypostasis of the Archons* in the Nag Hammadi library (no. 39, according to Doresse) is an abridgement of the *Book of Noria*. I am grateful to Jonathan Smith for drawing my attention to the translation of the *Hypostasis of the Archons* by J. Leipoldt and H. M. Schenke, *Koptisch-gnostische Schriften aus den Papyrus Codices von Nag 'Hammadi* (1960). Schenke denies the connection of this work with the *Book of Noria*, but more recent scholarship has affirmed the connection; see R. McL. Wilson, *Gnosis and the New Testament* (London, 1968), pp. 125 ff.

78. *Panarion* 26. 17. 1 ff., translation (slightly modified) by Benko, "The Libertine Gnostic Sect," pp. 109–10. The text was discussed by Leonhard Fendt, *Gnostische Mysterien: Ein Beitrag zur Geschichte des christlichen Gottesdienstes* (Munich, 1922), pp. 3–29, and by H. Leisegang, *La Gnose*, trans. Jean Gouillard (Paris, 1951), pp. 129–35; see also Alfonso M. di Nola, *Parole segrete di Gesù* (Turin, 1964), pp. 87–90, with more recent bibliographies. There are some other references to these practices of the Phibionites, the most important being *Pistis*

Sophia, chap. 147, and the *Second Book of Jeû*, chap. 43; cf. Benko, pp. 112–13. Thus, the sect existed at least a century before Epiphanius wrote his report. Some of the accounts of Epiphanius have been confirmed by the Nag Hammadi documents; cf. Doresse, *Les Livres secrets*, 1:282 (= *The Secret Books*, p. 250). See Benko, pp. 113 ff., for other Gnostic sects practicing similar sexual aberrations. Fendt pointed out (pp. 3–5) the liturgical characteristics of the orgiastic ceremonies described by Epiphanius, and Benko (pp. 114–19) convincingly argued its Christian presuppositions. One is least convinced, however, by Fendt's hypothesis of the Mother Goddess's influences (pp. 8 ff.).

79. Benko, "The Libertine Gnostic Sect," p. 117, summarizing *Panarion* 25. 2. 2 ff.

80. Ibid. One can see how the central Gnostic myth can be valorized differently; cf. the Manichaean interpretation above, p. 107.

81. *Panarion* 26. 5, translated in Benko, "The Libertine Gnostic Sect," p. 110.

82. One must also keep in mind that in the Greek translation of the Old Testament God's *pneuma* hovered over the waters; thus, the *pneuma hagion* was the divine sperm, generator of life; cf. Leisegang, *La Gnose*, p. 134, and esp. his *Pneuma Hagion* (Leipzig, 1922), pp. 71–72, where the Greek medical and philosophical conceptions are also discussed.

83. See R. B. Onians, *The Origins of European Thought* (Cambridge, Eng., 1951), p. 115.

84. Ibid., pp. 119–20.

85. See, *inter alia*, E. S. Drower, *The Secret Adam: A Study of Nasoraean Gnosis* (Oxford, 1960), pp. 15, 23–24, 76–77, etc. Cf. Kurt Rudolph, "Problems of a History of the Development of the Mandaean Religion," *History of Religions* 8 (1969): 210–35.

86. See, for instance, A. D. Nock and A.-J. Festugière, eds., *Corpus hermeticum*, 4 vols. (Paris, 1954), 1:4, 1:6, etc.; cf. A.-J. Festugière, *La Révélation d'Hermès Trismégiste*, 4 vols. (Paris, 1949–50), esp. 3: 106, 4: 241 ff.

87. See *Pistis Sophia*, quoted and discussed by Leisegang, *La Gnose*, pp. 242 ff.; cf. Doresse, *The Secret Books*, pp. 66 ff.

88. The equation of light and sperm was also known to the Sethians; see Hippolytus *Elenchos* V. XIX. 13–15. Cf. Irenaeus *Against Heresies* I. VII. 2 (Harvey, 1:118) apropos of Mark, the founder of the Marcosian sect, who proposed to a woman that she receive him sexually, as "the seed of light"; quoted and discussed by E. Goodenough, *Jewish Symbols in the Greco-Roman Period*, 6:103.

89. Cf. Doresse, *The Secret Books*, p. 146.

90. From the vast production of Henry Corbin, we may cite the following: *Avicenna and the Visionary Recital*, trans. Willard R. Trask (New York, 1960); *Creative Imagination in the Sufism of Ibn Arabi*, trans. Ralph Manheim (New York, 1969); "Terre céleste et Corps de Résurrection d'après quelques traditions iraniennes," *Eranos-Jahrbuch* 23 (1953): 151–250; "Physiologie de l'homme de lumière dans le soufisme iranien," in *Ombre et lumière* (Paris and Brussels, 1961), pp.

135–257. Of course, the Islamic light-theology has a Koranic source and justification; cf. *Koran* XXIV. 35: "God is the Light of Heaven and Earth . . . a Light over Light, etc."; see G.-C. Anawati and Louis Gardet, *Mystique musulmane* (Paris, 1961), pp. 56 ff.

91. Sohrawardi discusses the fifteen categories of photisms experienced by mystics; see Corbin, "Physiologie de l'homme de lumière," p. 186 and n. 62.

92. See ibid., pp. 186 ff. On the "Green Light," see ibid., pp. 199 ff.; on the "Dark Light," ibid., pp. 228 ff.

93. A somewhat similar situation seems to have characterized light-experiences in medieval Christian mysticism and alchemy. See Ernst Benz, *Die Vision: Erfahrungsformen und Bilderwelt* (Stuttgart, 1969), esp. pp. 94 ff., 326 ff.; cf. C. G. Jung, *Psychology and Alchemy*, trans. R. F. C. Hull, 2d ed. (Princeton, N.J., 1968); id., *Alchemical Studies*, trans. R. F. C. Hull (Princeton, N.J., 1967), s.v. "Light."

94. See M. Eliade, "South American High Gods, Part II," *History of Religions* 10, no. 3 (February 1971): 234–66, esp. pp. 261–59 and the bibliography quoted in n. 83. The main source is G. Reichel-Dolmatoff, *Desana: Simbolismo de los Indios Tukano del Vaupés* (Bogotá, 1968), now available in an English translation from the University of Chicago Press under the title *Amazonian Cosmos: The Sexual and Religious Symbolism of the Tukano Indians* (Chicago, 1971).

95. Reichel-Dolmatoff, *Desana*, pp. 31 ff.

96. Ibid., p. 72.

97. Ibid., p. 58; cf. also p. 33.

98. Reichel-Dolmatoff, "El contexto cultural de un alucinogeno aborigen: *Banisteriopsis Caapi*," *Revista de la Academia Colombiana de Ciencias Exactas, Físicas y Naturales* 13, no. 51 (Bogotá, 1969): 327–45, esp. p. 330.

99. See Reichel-Dolmatoff, *Desana*, p. 18, for the myth of the voyage; cf. pp. 40 ff.

100. Ibid., p. 20. Of course, the myth explains the origin of menstruation and the ritual fumigation of menstruating girls.

101. Ibid., p. 42.

102. Ibid., p. 46.

103. Ibid., p. 98.

104. Ibid., pp. 99–100.

105. Ibid., pp. 105 ff.

106. Reichel-Dolmatoff, "El contexto cultural," p. 331.

107. Ibid.

108. The women sing: "Beba, beba! Para eso hemos nacido! Beba, beba! Porque es de nuestro oficio. Bebiendo conozca todas las tradiciones de sus padres. Bebiendo tendrán valor. Nosotras les ayudamos!" (Reichel-Dolmatoff, *Desana*, p. 132).

109. Reichel-Dolmatoff, "El contexto cultural," p. 331. In every *yagé* plant the Desanas distinguish boughs or portions of different colors (green, red, white), which they relate to the color seen during the hallucinatory visions (ibid., p. 332). See also Michael J. Harner, "Common Themes in South American *Yagé* Experiences," in

Hallucinogens and Shamanism, ed. Michael J. Harner (New York, 1973), pp. 155–75; Claudio Narango, "Psychological Aspects of the *Yagé*," ibid., pp. 176–90.

110. Reichel-Dolmatoff, "El contexto cultural," p. 336.

111. Ibid., p. 335; cf. *Desana*, p. 132.

112. As yet we do not have a good monograph on the world mythology of hallucinogenic plants, i.e., one recording all the origin myths of such plants, their mythological personifications, the religious valorizations of hallucinatory visions, etc. See Marlene Dobkin del Rios, "The Non-Western Use of Hallucinatory Agents," in *Drug Use in America: Problem in Perspective* (Washington, D.C., 1973), 1:1179–1235.

113. But we must also add that the Desanas' spiritual world is a quite recent discovery of South American ethnology and, moreover, a discovery obtained through an exceptionally lucky accident; almost everything we know about their theological system is due to the chance encounter between Reichel-Dolmatoff and an intelligent Desana informant. It suffices to compare what we knew before the publication of Reichel-Dolmatoff's book with our present knowledge to realize the difference this discovery has made. It is doubtful that a similar discovery with regard to Gnostic and Tantric systems will ever occur.

114. See, *inter alia*, Max Knoll, "Die Welt der inneren Lichterscheinungen," *Eranos-Jahrbuch* 35 (1965): 361–97, with 42 figs.; see also the notes and bibliographies, pp. 393–96. For a psychological investigation of photic phenomena, see J. H. Schultz, *Das autogene Training* (Stuttgart, 1964), pp. 232 ff., 357. See also Gerald Oster, "Phosphenes," *Scientific American* 222 (February 1970): 82–87.

Index

Abhinavagupta, 100–101, 136 nn. 39, 41

Achilpas, 19–20, 28

Adamites, 89

Adams, Evangeline, "America's female Nostradamus," 59–60

Agni, 105

Ahura Mazdah, 104

Akiba, Rabbi, 29

Alchemy: Chinese, 55, 125 n. 15; Indian, 55

Algonquins, cosmological symbolism of, 26

Ambrose, Saint, 41

Ameša-Spenta, 108

Anamnesis: Australian and Platonic theories of, 2; historiographical, 19

Angkor, represents the World, 23–24

Antarjyotiḥ, "inner light," 95–97

Apsu, 27

Aquarius, Age of, 60, 127 n. 36

Arada. *See* Herodiada

Aranda, 30, 89

Archons, in Manichaeism, 106–7, 109

Astrology, contemporary craze for, 59–61

Ātman, and "inner light," 95–97

Australian males, life-crises of, 32

Axis mundi, 25 ff.

Barbelo, 110–11

Baudelaire, Charles, 52, 53

"Beginnings," beatitude of the, 89–92

Benandanti, the, and the fertility cult in Friule, 73–78, 129 nn. 18–25

Bergier, Jacques, 8–9

Blavatsky, Mme, and the Theosophical Society, 51, 66

Boddhicitta, 99

Bogomils, 87, 90

Bořoros, cosmology of, 20–21

Brahman, 96–97

Brancuşi, Constantin, 16, 31

Brethren of the Free Spirit, 86

Breton, André, 52, 53

Bruiningk, H. van, 77–78

Bruno, Giordano, and the Hermetic tradition, 56–57

Buddha, 99; supernatural lights associated with, 96–97

Buddhism, 133 nn. 14–19, 134 nn. 20–21

Cakravartin (cosmocrator), 24

Călușari (Romanian cathartic dancers), 81–84, 130 n. 40, 131 nn. 41–45; flag of, 81–82; initiation of, 81; relation of, to fairies, 81–82
Candrakirti, 99
Cathari, 87
Caul, *benandanti* born enveloped in, 74, 129 n. 14
Center of the world, symbolism of, 21 ff.
Cernunnos, 72
Chagall, Marc, 1
Chardin, Teilhard de, 11–13
Christ, in· Phibionites' ritual orgies, 110
Christians, accused of sex orgies, 87–88
Church: of All World, 62; of Light, 62; of Satan, 62, 126 n. 26
City-building reiterates cosmogony, 21 ff.
Coincidentia oppositorum, 45, 66
Combat, ceremonial. See *Benandanti; Călușari; Sântoaderi; Strigoi*
Corbin, Henry, 55, 114, 140 n. 90, 141 nn. 91–92
Cosmology, 20 ff.
Coven of thirteen, 72

Dakotas (Indian tribe), 26
Darkness (Matter), in Manichaeism, 106–8
Dasein, death as most proper potentiality of, 46
Daumal, René, 52, 53, 62
Dead, partake in the world of the living, 41 ff.
Death: as *coincidentia oppositorum*,44 ff.; as initiation, 38, 43; as most proper potentiality of *Dasein*, 46; mythologies of, 32 ff.; myths on origin of, 33 ff.
Dēnkart, 103–4, 137 n. 50

Desanas, 115–18, 141–42
Devil: and the *benandanti*, 76; Lithuanian werewolves claim to fight the, 77–78; present at "heretical" orgies, 86–88
Devil-worshipers, accusation of being, 85–92
Diana (Roman goddess), 75, 79, 130 n. 39; her name became *zîna*, "fairy," in Romanian, 80; "Troop of," 78 ff.
Dianism, Dianus, 72
Dyaks, 30, 89; cosmogony and symbolism of, 25
Dziana, 80. See also Diana

Egyptian esotericism, 56–57
Eibschutz, Jonathan, 29
Ellwood, Robert, 62–63
Epiphanius, on the Gnostic sect of the Phibionites, 110–11
Esoteric doctrines and contemporary scholarship, 54–58
Esotericism, definition of, 48
"Extinction of lamps," 85–88

Fairies, 80–84. See also Diana; *Zîne*
Fali, house symbolism of the, 26
Feraferia, 62–63
Flag, of the *Călușari*, 81–82
Foucard, G., on Nilus' description of Arabian sacrifice, 7
France, Anatole, 50–51
Fraša (Renovation), 104
Fraticelli, 87
Freemasonry, occult, 55 ff.
Freud, Sigmund, 53; on the "totemic banquet," 4–5
Funerary: "geography," 38 ff.; rites, cosmological symbolism of, 35 ff.

Gandhāra, 101–2
Geographies, mythic and funerary, 42 ff.

Gētē, 108
Ginsburg, Carlo, 58, 78
Gnoli, Gherardo, 105, 108, 137–39
Gnosticism, 42, 108–9, 113, 139 nn.
    76–77; Jewish, 54
Gnostics, 87, 102, 105
Golden Bough, The, 5, 72
Gordon, A. D., 29
Guaita, Stanislas de, 50–52
Guénon, René, 51, 52, 65–67, 127 nn.
    39–41
Guhyasamāja Tantra, 99–100

Hallucinogenic visions, compared with
    sexual act, 116
Haoma, 104–5
Heidegger, Martin, 45 ff., 123 nn.
    22–24
Heimarmene, 108
Heresy trials, 70
"Heretics," accused of blasphemous
    orgies, 86–87
Hermetic texts, 56–57
Herodiada, Romanian, 81 ff.
Heussi, Karl, 7
Höfler, Otto, 73, 77
Homo religiosus, 30
Horoscopes, 59–61
Horse-men. *See Călușari; Sântoaderi*
House, at the Center of the World, 24
    ff.
Huysmans, J.-K., 51

Imago mundi, 23 ff.
Indonesian: myth on the origin of
    death, 34; religious symbolism, 25
Initiation, death as, 38
Ionesco, Eugène, 1–2, 14
Irodiada. *See* Herodiada
Israel, the sacred land, 27 ff.

Jerusalem: built at the Center of the
    World, 27–28; symbolism of, 28 ff.
Jewish Gnosticism, 54

Jīvan-mukta, 103
Joyce, James, 2

Kabbalah, 54
Kobrâ, Najmoddîn, 114
Kogi funerary rites and symbolism, 36
    ff.
Kore, the divine maiden, in Feraferia,
    63
Kumú, Desana priests, 115–18
Kuṇḍagolaka, 100–102, 112

LaVey, Anton, founder of Church of
    Satan, 61–62, 126 n. 29
Lea, Henry Charles, 57, 70–71
Leisegang, H., 111–12, 139 n. 78, 140
    n. 82
Lévi, Eliphas, 49
Lévi-Strauss, Claude, 13–16, 20, 121
    n. 15
Light, captive, in Manichaeism, 106–8
Light, as having the character of semen
    among the Desana, 115–17
Light, inner, 132 n. 1. See also *Antar-
    jyotih*
Light, mystical, 93 ff.; in ancient In-
    dia, 95–97; in ancient Iran, 103–5;
    among the Desana, 115–17; in Tan-
    trism, 98–103. *See also* Mystical
    light
Līlā, ceremonial "play," 100, 133 n.
    14
Logos spermatikos, 112
Lorca, Garcia, 3
Lucerna extincta, 85–88
Lycanthropy in seventeenth-century
    Lithuania, 77–78

Mādhyamika, 103
Maga, the state of, 108, 138 n. 71
Mahāvīra, supernatural light at birth
    of, 96
Maithuna, 99–103, 112, 136 n. 39

Mallarmé, Stéphane, 3, 53
Máma, Kogi shaman, 36
Manichaeans, 87
Manichaeism, 99–100, 105–9, 113, 135 n. 33, 138 nn. 67–69
Martinist Order, 50
Masonic lodges, 50
Masson, J. L., 136 nn. 39, 41
Menes, Thomas, famous astrologer, 60
Mēnōk, 108
Meru, Mount, 24
Messalians, 87
Mithra, 104
"Mixture" (*gumeščin*), 108–9
Model, cosmogonic, 21 ff.
Molé, Marijan, 137 n. 50, 138 nn. 57–58
Mommsen, Theodore, 18–19
Montanists, 87
Montgomery, Ruth (*A Gift of Prophecy*), 60
Morin, Edgar, 60–61
Multilocation of the departed soul, 40 ff.
Murray, Margaret, and theory of origin of Western witchcraft, 57–58, 71–73
Mystical light, 93 ff.; in ancient India, 95–97; in Chinese traditions, 134 n. 22; in Hellenistic times, 139 n. 75; in Tantrism, 99–100; in Tibet and among the Mongols, 98, 134 nn. 25–27. *See also* Light, mystical
Mystical lights, five, 100

Needham, Joseph, 55
Nerval, Gerard de, 2
Nilus' description of the sacrifice of a camel, 6–8
Nirvāṇa, 97
Nostalgias of contemporary Western man, 16–17
Novalis, Friedrich, 3
Numbakula, 20

Occult: "explosion," most recent, 58–63; revival, literature on, 124 n. 1; tradition, 55 ff.
Occultism: definition of, 48; interest of nineteenth-century French writers in, 49 ff.
Orgies, ritual, 88–90, 131 n. 62
Orphism, 42

Padma (womb), 99
Palestine as sacred land, 28 ff.
Papus, pseudonym of Dr. Encausse, 50–52
Paraphrase of Shem, 113
Pasqually, Martinus of, 50
Patwardhan, M. V., 136 nn. 39, 41
Paulicians, 87
Pauwels, Louis, 8–9
Payé, Desana shaman, 115–17
Péladan, Joseph, 50
Phaedrus, 18–19
Phibionites, and sanctification through semen, 109–12
Photisms, 119, 142 n. 114; morphology of, 112–14
"Pillar of the World," symbolism of, 25 ff.
Planète, 8–10
Platonism, 42
Pneuma, 109, 112–13
Polestar, 24
Psyche, identified with *sperma*, 112

Rāsamaṇḍalī, 88
Reformists, charged with holding sex orgies, 86–87
Reichel-Dolmatoff, G., 115–17, 123 n. 9, 141 nn. 94–109, 142 nn. 110–11; on symbolism of Kogi burial, 36–37
Religions, cosmic and historical, compared, 30–31

Renovatio, contemporary hope for, 63–65

Rimbaud, A., 52

Romanian parallels to *benandanti*, 78 ff.

Rome, foundation of, 22–23

Rose, Elliot, on Margaret Murray's theory, 72

Russell, J. B., 128 nn. 1, 5, 129 nn. 9, 25, 130 nn. 33, 39, 131 nn. 49, 50–57

Sabbath, 71, 75, 76

Sacral kingship in Iran, 137 n. 56

Saint-Martin, Louis-Claude de, the "Philosophe Inconnu," 50

Śakti, 99

Saṃsāra, 103

Sântoaderi, 82–84, 131 n. 46

Sartre, J.-P., 9–11, 61

Satan, Church of, 62

Scholem, Gershom, 54–55

"Secret languages," 136 n. 40

Seed, identified with spirit and light: in ancient India, 94–97; in Tibet, 98

Semen, sanctification through, among Phibionites, 109–12

Semen virile, 95–96, 113

"Separation" of spiritual essence from corporeal being, 108–9

Sexuality, demonization of, 90

Sexual intercourse in Tantrism, 99–103

Shamans, 38–39, 115–17; Kogi, 36–37

Shamanism, 56

Sioux, cosmological symbolism of, 26

Śiva, 99

Sivin, Nathan, 55

Smith, Jonathan Z., 28–29

Smith, W. Robertson, on Nilus' description of Arabian sacrifice, 6

Soma, 104–5

Sorcerers (*stregoni, strighe*), 74–78

Space, sacred, i.e., "real," 21 ff.; oriented, 30

Spirit, identified with light and seed: in ancient India, 94–97; in Tibet, 98

Stregoni, 74–78

Strighe, 74–78, 79

Strigoi, 79–80, 130 n. 33

Structuralism, 13–16

Sulcus primigenius, 22

Summers, Montague, 70

"Sun-Father," of the Desanas, 114–18

Svar, 104

Symbolism, Chinese, 25 ff.

Tantrāloka, 100–101, 136 nn. 39, 42

Tantrism, 55–56, 100–103, 136 nn. 38–42, 137 nn. 43–46; orgies in, 88

Tathāgatagarbha, identified with "luminous thought," 97, 134 n. 21.

Tehom, 27–28

Temple of Jerusalem, 28, 30

Theodore, Saint, patron of *Sântoaderi*, 82–84

Tibet, 98 ff.

Tiryakian, E. A., 48, 124 nn. 1–3, 11

Totality, primordial, 89–90

Totem and Taboo (Freud), 3–5

Ts'on k'a pa, 99

Tucci, Giuseppe, 99, 102, 113, 135 nn. 30–33, 136 n. 42, 137 nn. 43–46

Upanishads, 102, 113, 137 nn. 8–9; solar seed in the, 95–97

Uṣṇīṣa, 133 n. 14

Vajra (*membrum virile*), 99

Valéry, Paul, 3

Vallabhācāryas, 88

Verlaine, Paul, 52

Verne, Jules, 2

Vouru.kaša Sea, 104–5

Waldensians, 86

Warner, W. Lloyd, 32, 40

Wellhausen, J., 6
Werewolves, Lithuanian, fight the Devil, 77–78
Wilde Heer, 130 n. 34
Witchcraft, European: bibliography on, 128 nn. 1–8; theories on origins of, 57 ff., 69–73
Xvarenah, 103–5

Yagé, 116–18
Yasna as promoting "separation" of spiritual essence from corporeal being, 108
Yates, Frances A., 56–57
Yeats, W. B., and the Order of the Golden Dawn, 51
Yoga, 55–56

Zarathustra, 103–4
Zātspram, 104
Zîne, 80–82, 130 n. 35. *See also* Diana
Zoroastrianism, 42, 108–9